D1474157

Also by Sharon L. Stohrer
Published by Routledge Press:

THE SINGER'S COMPANION

The Performer's Companion

A Guide to Conquering Performance Anxiety

Sharon L. Stohrer

Diana McCullough, contributing writer

Chapter 10 illustrations by Ron Boisvert, MSMI, MSID

CreateSpace Books

CreateSpace
ISBN-13:
978-1500799472

ISBN-10:
1500799475

To the Performer in All of Us

CONTENTS

ACKNOWLEDGEMENTS

Thanks to former voice student, Edek Sher, for allowing me to reproduce his character analysis as a model. I am grateful to Dr. Karl Paulnack for permission to reprint parts of his eloquent speech about the importance of music and music-making. Diana McCullough is a most cherished colleague, workshop partner and contributor to this book--she and her talents are much appreciated. Many thanks to Molly Kathleen and Karen Linden for technical assistance. For general support, encouragement and editorial help, I am grateful to my loving husband, David Rives, and to Susan Boisvert, Diane Cushing, and Susan Hermance Fedak.

PREFACE

Did you know that performance anxiety is the number one fear in this country, according to several studies, with performance "failure" feared by many people more than death?! Even so, folks are often reluctant to speak of it, believing that they are alone, that something is wrong with them, or that fellow performers or speakers do not share their struggles.

Further compounding the problem, manifestations of stage fright are rarely the same from person to person and the degree of performance anxiety can vary. Some suffer to such an extent that their symptoms are identical to full-blown panic attacks. Most of these people think it is their fault somehow—so they simply refuse to perform or conveniently become ill around performance time. On the other end are those who have just a vague feeling of discomfort or a sensation of being stiff. These individuals often assume this "goes with the territory" so they give performances that are perhaps adequate, but lack the sparkle and zest that could be theirs, were they to free themselves of nervousness.

Based on insights gained through years of one-on-one work with performers and workshops with groups of all sizes, this book is aimed at both ends of that spectrum, as well as everyone in between. You will discover simple, effective techniques and exercises that can be practiced just as the music is practiced, requiring only a few minutes each day.

Chapter One

THE DEEP DARK SECRET

"If we knew each other's secrets, what comforts we should find."-
- John Churton Collins

If you suffer from performance anxiety, you likely think that you are alone and somehow deeply flawed. Even awareness of fellow students or colleagues who experience stage fright is no comfort, because your operative belief is, "Well, not as much as I do." So a feeling of isolation becomes the norm along with not talking about it and not dealing with it. The belief that performance anxiety results from defects of character turns it into **a deep dark secret**. Because it is an uncomfortable subject to think about, those afflicted usually do not face it until the last second, literally, when nerves have taken over, and it is too late to do much about it.

Many performers give up a fair amount of personal empowerment in the belief that good outings are due to fate, alignment of the stars, appeasing the gods and so on. Just take a look sometime at dressing rooms in theatres or concert halls to see all the tokens of superstition: the lucky objects or clothing, the rituals involved prior to curtain, the special words used (such as "break a leg" or "toi, toi, toi" because it is bad luck to say "good luck" and for heaven's sake, DON'T mention the play *Macbeth*) and on and on and on. Another example is the common fear that a good dress rehearsal will mean a poor performance. Nonsense! The reason that shaky dress rehearsals are followed by good performances is because the experience of that bad rehearsal has motivated the participants to review scores or scripts, fully prepare and take nothing for granted. The truth is that good rehearsals usually precede good performances—we normally do what we have practiced.

Another pitfall in overcoming performance anxiety is the quest for THE magic answer: just find the right mantra, or mental strategy or medication, and all will be just fine. Along with this is the assumption that performers with confidence and poise come by that genetically. While there are some folks who are naturally more at home on the stage, the majority have to work for confidence and ease. All musicians get the jitters from time to time, depending on how important the performance is. The difference between those who are debilitated by their nerves and those who are able to perform well is that the latter prepare far in advance and have made performing techniques (meditation, affirmations, visualization, score study, and so forth) a regular part of their practicing and preparation.

The actual symptoms of performance anxiety can differ widely from person to person and from event to event—so no one answer, no "silver bullet" is going to solve the challenge for everyone every time. Some folks get dry mouth, butterflies, shaky knees, trembling fingers, others have increased heart rate, muscle tension, sweating, many musicians become nauseated or need to go frequently to the toilet and often have high, shallow breathing. Even more troubling are the mental symptoms of distraction, a sense of impending doom, feelings of panic, negative self-talk, and memory blanks.

The sad reality is that musicians are under ever-increasing pressure. The concert-going public generally expects the kind of flawless performance found on commercial recordings, in which the studio has edited out any mistakes. In most places people make their own music far less often than in years past and tend to put those who do perform on pedestals—expecting perfection. In the past, people used to sing while doing the dishes or other chores—now they often put on the radio or a recording. It was also more common in decades past for families and friends to have frequent, informal times of music making, whether gathering around the piano, singing in the car, getting out guitars or participating in a string quartet. All of these activities meant that the public in general realized that mistakes are inevitable and that aspiring professionals had many more opportunities to test their mettle before going on to higher stakes performances.

Along with the pressure of flawless recordings is the reality of fewer and fewer public performance opportunities. In his book, *Who Killed Classical Music,* Norman Lebrecht describes how our culture has made the music world into a cult of hero worship: only a few divas and divos are able to make their living as performers, with far fewer regional orchestras, concert series and opera companies. When a particular city brings a superstar musician to perform, that event uses money from arts foundations and government grants that otherwise would have funded a <u>great number</u> of performances by <u>regional</u> artists, chamber groups, and aspiring professionals. Therefore, there are fewer performance opportunities at the intermediate level, and many more people vying for them.

The realities of music making as a livelihood or even an avocation can be harsh, yet more and more people study and perform every year. There is something deeply satisfying to our souls, or we would not invest the time and the money. So if a musician struggles with stage fright, learning to overcome the jitters and use the adrenaline is vital to survive in today's realities of fewer opportunities and expectations of perfection.

One other benefit from facing performance anxiety is the opportunity to delve deeply and heal wounds that were usually first suffered in childhood, whether at home, in school or at play. None of us gets through childhood without scars. I often tell participants in my workshops that, despite its over-exposure in books and other media, the concept of embracing one's inner child is helpful here. Look on overcoming performance anxiety as a time of experimentation—taking that scared little girl or little boy by the hand and seeing what might be helpful to her or him at this rehearsal or in this performance. The very fact that you suffer from performance anxiety <u>can</u> be indicative of a more sensitive nature and one that is concerned with the thoughts and reactions of others. What we want to do, via all the steps outlined in this book, is to allow that sensitivity to flourish without being constrained by fear.

When presenting workshops on conquering performance anxiety, I can often sense the expectation from participants that I will give them that one special mantra or technique or mental attitude that will take away all their nervousness. Invariably, faces fall as I describe the preparations involved in performing with confidence. I heard that same phenomenon recently while listening to the popular NPR news/humor program, *Wait, Wait, Don't Tell Me!* The guest was Pete Carroll who is now the head coach of the Seattle Seahawks. (Previously Mr. Carroll coached football for nine years at the University of Southern California, where they won seven PAC 10 titles and two national championships. He also recently published a book entitled <u>Win Forever</u>.) The host, Peter Sagal, asked the question that, in other words, is on the lips of most performance anxiety workshop attendees: "What can you say to make them give that extra mile?" Mr. Carroll replied, "It's about the preparation during the week that gets you ready to play. When you have guys that have put in their work, that have done their studying, the idea is to get them to feel they don't have to worry about what's going to happen, they've been so well prepared. . .It isn't about the last words you say, it's more the release that you give them to freely play because they're so prepared, they're so jacked up." And that, Dear Reader, is the thrust of this book: to give you enough techniques and methods that you will be musically, physically, mentally and psychologically ready to perform, along with a few mental strategies to help you get "jacked up."

My Own Story

I studied music in college (around the time the earth cooled) long before there were books and workshops available on overcoming stage fright. People rarely discussed nervousness and teachers almost never dealt with it, so we students were left to figure it out ourselves. Most of my fellow students had manageable levels of stage fright, or they turned to ingesting substances, or they struggled through the required performances in order to graduate and then put their singing aside or their instrument on the shelf. I took voice lessons here and there and I knew deep down that I had far more talent for singing than for piano, but I also realized at some level that I felt way too vulnerable when singing onstage. As I did at the piano, really. So I hid behind accompanying others: that way I could be seen and perform, and yet not be in the spotlight. (This is not to malign accompanists: the art of collaboration is one to be admired. In my case, though, it was hiding.) Chamber music performances and accompanying also felt somewhat supportive, in that by making music with others, I would not be singled out for a great deal of praise, but, most importantly, I would avoid much scrutiny and judgment.

I remember so well thinking that something was terribly wrong with me. Although I did have some enjoyable performing experiences, my lack of confidence led me to initially pursue graduate work in music history and theory—removing myself further from the "hot seat" so to speak. Since that pursuit was a substitute and not my real desire, I did not last more than one term. Floundering for many years and trying to find my life's work, at the urging of a friend, I finally began regular voice lessons at age 30 and it changed my life.

It was not as if someone flicked on a light switch, the change and illumination were more gradual, like a dimmer switch: it took some time to realize that I had truly "come home." All kinds of things started to make sense in new ways. I loved languages, poetry, drama, and bodywork—all of which are essential to singers. I was a late bloomer, for sure, but happy to finally find my passion. Now, however, I had to face performance anxiety with no hiding allowed.

I did give recitals and concerts, some of which were relatively relaxed and enjoyable experiences. Those usually involved other performers and I felt a sense of support and camaraderie. Others, especially solo recitals, were terrible ordeals and I got a heavier feeling of dread in my gut as the date approached. Part of me wanted to perform; I did NOT want to give up, yet I suffered anxiety to the level of full-blown panic attacks. I would have difficulty sleeping; I would endure headaches, pins-and-needles, hyperventilation; I would feel

13

detached from other people and my thoughts would race; I would experience a strong sense of doom every time I heard a friend say they looked forward to the performance, and a great amount of body tension that increased as the date neared. I did not mentally "hear" critical voices, but sensed them and that translated into body tension. I was hypersensitive to criticism and suggestions, fearing that everyone was my judge and jury and certainly thinking the worst about my abilities and me.

On the actual performance day, I would have trouble breathing deeply; I would shake, have sweaty palms, dry mouth, butterflies, and take lots of trips to the bathroom. I would find it very difficult to focus, to fully inhabit my body and feel any sense of being grounded, or sense having power or energy, or expansion of my posture. It truly was a torment. Even good outings did not build my confidence for future performances. I believed that those achievements were when I cheated fate, not realizing that my preparations had given me a solid framework. At the same time, I did not trust myself to replicate and build on my successes. I think the only thing that kept me going was the strong belief at a visceral level that singing was right for me.

Luckily by then there were some books available on stage fright. So I read some and did the exercises in them and went to a workshop on overcoming performance anxiety and tried all the techniques. Fortunately I was also in therapy for work on some relationship problems and it became clear that, in my case, performance anxiety was symptomatic of some deeper psychological material requiring attention. So I delved into psychotherapy and worked very hard on my own issues. Voice lessons and therapy and working on performance anxiety techniques for a couple of years all resulted in a healthier, happier person who was ready to perform. I went on to graduate school in vocal performance and a career as a teacher, performer, church musician and workshop facilitator.

As my teaching career unfolded, I frequently encountered students who suffered from stage fright. For some, the nerves did not become a problem until their senior or graduate recitals. For others, the very first time performing for their college or university peers was enough to scare them silly. I worked one on one with my own voice students and then more and more regularly with students of other faculty members. Eventually I started offering small seminars and workshops on conquering performance anxiety, and began to branch out to other schools and organizations.

I love to perform and to help others overcome their anxiety, but I am neither a trained psychologist nor a therapist. So while I do advocate some inner dialogue and self-programming, I focus instead on preparation: simple steps that only add a few minutes to your daily practice routine.

I always begin my workshops by asking participants to think of overcoming stage fright as a journey, a process, and an exploration. For some, it may require the kind of intense work and longevity that my own path took. For most, a few minutes daily for a few weeks to a few months of exercises, techniques and reading will do the trick. There are no guarantees how long or involved your process will be, but please vow to start your journey today. You deserve to succeed! So let us explore techniques and methods that prepare you to be musically, physically, mentally and psychologically ready to perform, along with a few mental strategies to help you get "jacked up" and "in the zone!"

Chapter Two

MENTAL PREPARATION

"...take the focus of your attention away from thinking and direct it into the body, where Being can be felt ..."
--Eckhart Tolle

A common cliché about performing among musicians is that it is 90% psychological. There is a lot of truth to that adage. Just as athletes must get their minds around the game, so, too, do musicians grow in performance ease with mental strategies and attitudes.

Classical Singer magazine interviewed the international opera star, Frederica von Stade, a few years ago. She is known for her superb acting ability along with a glorious voice and is generally considered one of the kindest, most down-to-earth singers in the business. In the article she said many interesting things about her own singing, performing and preparation. My favorite was her observation that a singer's job (*) is to tell stories and move audiences and that anything else is a distraction or external. She gave examples of distractions and externals as these kind of thoughts: "Oh, so and so is here and the last time he heard me I didn't sing very well, so I MUST be great today!" or "Ah, this conductor is in the audience and I really want her to hire me, so I've got to nail this." I would add that distractions and externals include audience sounds and bodily sensations such as dry mouth, butterflies, and shaky knees.

Here is the rub: the problem with dry mouth, butterflies and shaky knees is that we start to focus on them rather than the task at hand. It quickly becomes a spiral of fear with thoughts such as, "Oh my god, my knees are shaking, how can I ever stay grounded and play?! Now I know I won't do well, why am I here? Oh, this is horrible! And so forth."

These mind spirals are the reason that people with fear of flying are often seen on airplanes flicking their wrists with rubber bands or watch bands—because that tiny bit of pain gets them back in their bodies, in the moment, and out of the mind-racing cycle of fear. In western culture we spend a great deal of time living in our heads, especially in logical, rational and analytical thought, and very little time fully inhabiting our bodies. One way to avoid these cycles of fear is to work on living in the moment and staying in your body. Some aids to that end are meditation, bodywork, sensory practice (please see Chapter Five) and focus.

* Instrumentalists also tell stories, although normally in abstract. You may find it helpful to write an actual poem or story to your music, and have someone in mind to whom you are speaking or for whom you are playing.

TIP: What we focus on increases!

Often performers will find ways to distract themselves from the fear they feel or the symptoms they are experiencing. While this may work for some occasions, it cannot work forever: eventually you will feel the fear and/or be unnerved by the shaky legs, dry mouth or butterflies. What I suggest is gradually learning to face the fear, embrace the symptoms, and discover how to perform and even have peak experiences with them. For that to happen, focus is necessary.

The ability to focus is quickly becoming a challenge in our multi-tasking society, along with patience for learning things that require a process, or an unfolding. Most high school and college- aged musicians I know are the masters of multi-tasking: texting, eating, listening to music, and talking with friends—all at once. This ability has its merits, yet the capacity to focus by these multi-taskers is diminishing. The good news is that focus for performing can be learned, and I am a prime example of that.

I find it almost impossible to concentrate when trying to read on commuter trains while folks are having loud cell phone conversations, or staying with the movie when someone behind me is noisily crunching a snack. However, I have often met with audience members after performing in recitals or concerts and have heard that the squeak of the piano's sustaining pedal was driving them nuts, or a baby's cry or some other distraction – I did not hear it at all! So if I, who am so easily distracted in everyday life, can learn to focus on stage, so can you!

LEARNING FOCUS

✳ The first step is to use a technique from the performance anxiety expert, Don Greene (please see Resources Section for his books.) He suggests that you take a candle, light it, and for sixty seconds stare at the flame – not the wick, not the candle, not the table that it is on. Your eyes and your attention might want to wander, and if they do, just acknowledge that you have lost the focus, and gently bring your attention back – it is counterproductive to become angry or frustrated. A minute may seem like a short time, until you try it! Practice this visual focus exercise for a week, or at least a few days.

✳ The second approach is kinesthetic—easiest to focus on your breathing –not only the breath coming into the body, but also the sense of expansion and the breath leaving again. This may begin to feel calming and meditative—all to the good.

✳ Then move on to using that minute to focus aurally. Find one sound in the room (there are usually several: the clock ticking, the ventilation, your own breath) and see if you can focus on it to the exclusion of other stimuli, and try that for several days.

✳ In performance, we want visual, kinesthetic and auditory foci, so the next step is to experiment with these focal points in practice and rehearsal. You can certainly decide for yourself whether you want to do it for all or a portion of your practice or rehearsal time. It is helpful, at first, to let go of technical and interpretive expectations. Look on developing focus as another technical ability, a type of coordination similar to other technical skills you have attained. Often when working to acquire such new skills, we must release our expectations of expression and performance for a short time until that new ability is mastered. As with working on focus itself, you might want to start with visual focus. For singers this is your "other"— to whom you are singing (please see Chapter Three for complete character and scene preparation ideas). That "other" may change in the course of a song or aria: you might begin by focusing on the moon and then transition to singing to another person, and so forth. Move your focus slowly, in time with the music or the interlude and practice staying with that visual focus as if your life depended on it! Even if the walls were to fall, you would still be focused. For reasons of singing technique, you do not want a focal point to be too high or low, but it also need not be center – you may certainly look slightly right or left of center, and you can experiment. For a few practice sessions, focus primarily on the visual, ignoring other elements.

If you are an instrumentalist, visual focus may depend on the situation. If you are using a score, you can practice feeling pulled into it, allowing the printed page to keep your full attention, as if experiencing tunnel vision. You probably will want to look up from time to time, so you will need to find a focal point just a singer does. If you are playing from memory, you might change focus, depending on changes of mood within the piece. Perhaps invent a storyline for your piece and a character for yourself.

❋ After you have explored the visual focus for a few days, practice focusing on your breath, whether or not you use air to make your music. To the exclusion of other stimuli, notice how low the breath goes in your body— feel the expansion of ribs and abdominal muscles – notice the feeling of the air in your throat as you exhale. Strive to keep this inward kinesthetic awareness as you play or sing. You may find that deep breathing is not enough to make you fully inhabit your body—especially if you do not use air to play your instrument. In that case, you might also experiment with:

- Imagine playing from the soles of your feet.
- Play from your core – your solar plexus.
- Feel as if you are dancing with your instrument.
- Sense what temperature is the small of your back.
- Imagine that the strings/keyboard/keys are velvet.
- Notice what temperature is the back of your knees.
- Feel as if your whole body is playing your instrument.

❋ The third area of focus is the next to work on in your practice or rehearsal sessions. Before you start to sing or play, hear the first few measures of music exactly the way you would like them to sound. Even when what comes out of your mouth or your instrument does not match that ideal, stay with it and eventually, with practice, the two will merge.

❋ Having tried all three areas of focus, now begin to combine two at a time, until you can get all three going. Focusing our attention on these three areas is our version of the athlete's focus-- "keep your eye on the ball." It is also similar to the self-talk you see in runners or swimmers just before a competition.

❋ After some practice with focus, recruit a friend or colleague to make noise or other distractions while you perform in rehearsal. The goal is to allow the distractions to be there without disturbing your flow, do not try to tune them out. Practice your areas of focus as if your life depended on it.

TIP: The ability to focus will grow with repetition!

If, in rehearsal or performance, you are truly able to focus on your breath, your sound and your "other" you will not have time to think about shaky knees and butterflies and <u>because you are not worried about them</u>, they go away! Allowing them to be there: acknowledging, for example, that your legs are shaking but then bringing your attention back to your focus areas will stop the fear spiral and allow your body and mind to relax.

In her book, *A Soprano on Her Head*, Eloise Ristad suggests that you attempt to increase whatever symptom is bothering you. Shaky legs? Try to make it worse. Dry mouth? Imagine you are swabbing your mouth with cotton. As counter-intuitive as it seems, having no fear of the symptoms, letting them be there—even encouraging them, will ensure that they go away. I think her suggestion of increasing them is great to use in informal performances and rehearsals. For actual performances, I would suggest gentle self-talk: "Okay, my legs are shaking. That makes me feel scared about losing my sense of grounding. But I know from practice that if I go back to my areas of focus, I'll be fine. So let's breathe deeply and get back to visual and auditory focus." The eventual goal is to have the areas of focus become automatic in all your practicing, rehearsing and performing—helping you to ease more reliably and more easily into the Zone– the flow, what some call peak performances, (please see Chapter Eight).

This focus, the musician's equivalent of "keep your eye on the ball" is important no matter how any particular piece or program is unfolding. So often, the moment that a performer thinks, "Oh, this is going great!" they then make a mistake or lose the momentum of the piece. Thinking about whether the music is unfolding well or not is stepping outside the flow, outside the focus and is certain to undermine all your careful preparation.

NARROW FOCUS AND WIDE FOCUS

In recitals, we can keep the focus narrow on our bodies (breathing) our "other" and our ideal sound. Since these are normally the venues for beginning performers, it is wise to spend a fair amount of time on learning narrow focus. Eventually, there will be situations where a wider focus is needed:

- Working with a conductor
- Playing in a trio, quartet, or other ensemble
- Singing a song that is comic, narrative, or directed to the audience
- Accompanying at the piano, harpsichord, guitar or organ
- Working with an orchestra

Once you feel that your narrow focus is reliable, it would be smart to start including more than one visual focus. Just as you have practiced, step-wise, all the ways of focusing, start with just two foci --then try three. The ideal, over time, is to play or sing in a way that is more inclusive of the audience. Be patient with yourself and if, in a given rehearsal or performance, this wider focus makes your confidence sink; pull the attention back to breathing and a narrower focus. Learning to stay grounded and undistracted with a wider focus can take several months to do.

FEAR

Workshop participants often ask me about fear, as if it is all-powerful, a monster that will track you down and devour you. Believe it or not, a bit of fear can be your friend! If we are too relaxed, too placid, then we risk performances that are bland, that lack some "zing." While we do not want to be so scared that we are tied up in knots, neither can we be completely relaxed—a bit of fear can translate into excitement, adrenaline, the "edge" that performers need. So embrace your fear: feel it. It will **not** kill you and being afraid does not mean you are unable to perform! Enjoy the rush, but keep your eyes on the ball! The performer's equivalent of keeping your eyes on the ball, is to go back to your focal points and to practice the gentle self-talk mentioned above.

On the television show, *Inside the Actor's Studio*, the actor Al Pacino was asked what it was like, in the movie, *Scent of a Woman*, to play a blind character. He said,

> "It frees you in some way; it focuses you on other things. That's the whole idea, to be so focused on other things that it frees you in some strange way. Free yourself. Free yourself. As Michelangelo once said, 'Lord, free me of myself so I can please you.' I think that basically what you're trying to do it to get yourself out of the way all the time. And when you're very successful at something--that's when you do that the most."

So focusing on the here and now by staying with a visual, auditory and kinesthetic focus will help free you in many ways to invent, to experiment and to unleash your creativity. Other helps for attaining peak performance are relaxation techniques, visualization exercises and affirmations.

RELAXATION TECHNIQUES

In order to avoid the spirals of fear, it is paramount to learn mindfulness, living in your body (rather than your head) and living in the moment. As mentioned before, this is all quite alien to contemporary western culture—so we must seek out opportunities to learn moment-by-moment living. Not only are relaxation techniques helpful in preparing to perform, they also nourish the soul and the artist within. The musician's life is one of challenge and discipline often characterized by great sacrifices. So take the time to give back to yourself—nourish

23

yourself in as many spiritual ways as possible. We are not alone in living with great discipline, challenge and sacrifice—many athletes do as well. The difference is that they make no excuses about needing every tool at their disposal to perform well—most engage in some kind of relaxation technique, whether it is Yoga or Tai Chi or Qi Dong or meditation. Often musicians are hard on themselves, thinking that they should just be able to perform without help.

There is an adage that is apt here: the voice mirrors the soul. (For instrumentalists—one's music mirrors one's soul). While there are many reasons for performance anxiety, the one ever-increasing source is daily anxiety. We live in uncertain times economically, politically and socially—we live in a time of terrorism. Added to that is the pressure of ever-increasing speeds of communication, including the necessity of checking voice mail, Facebook, tweets, text messages, and often several email accounts. On top of these general western society demands are unique musical stressors of performance standards based on studio "cleansed" recordings, rising concert pitch in orchestras (especially hard for singers) and the increasing expectation of performance artists to be not only talented and adept at performing but also gregarious in interviews, outgoing in general and blessed with movie star looks. If you are a high-school or college student, you also have to balance the artist's life with deadlines and coursework. With all that tension, taking some time in daily life to work on de-stressing is vital. If you go about your daily life highly stressed, you cannot help but bring that into your performing.

Investigate taking lessons or classes in Yoga, Centergy, Tai Chi, Qi Dong, Reiki, or Meditation. (See the Resources section for websites and other information). It is important that whichever method you choose, you make it a habitual part of your life. If you wait until just a few weeks before a performance to try one of these techniques, you will not have had regular, sustained practice in moment-by-moment living, and it will be harder to transfer that to the stage. The benefit of memory is helpful as well. For example, I like to do some Hatha Yoga postures (asanas) backstage, not only because they help me feel grounded and expanded, but also because doing so brings back memories of Yoga class, which is a very relaxing and pleasurable experience. So if I am a little too excited or a little nervous (and they truly are flip sides of the same coin), the experience of doing the asanas as well as the pleasurable memories they evoke will help get me in that optimal arousal state. And that is key: an optimal arousal state. You probably would be <u>too</u> relaxed if you did, for example, a Yoga deep relaxation just before performing. Ideally, deep relaxation should be a regular part of your weekly schedule, with just visualizations or affirmations as a backstage possibility.

After workshops, participants have often said something like, "I don't get too nervous, but I'm never as calm onstage as I am when I'm just jamming with friends." You are not supposed to be! The goal is not to be easy and comfy—think of your performing as a challenge, like a race. You rarely hear marathon runners cheerily saying "I'm going to have so much FUN at the race on Saturday!" Yet running the race clearly has its rewards, or they would not do it. Your performing is like that race: a challenge, often marathon-like, with a great sense of satisfaction and reward-- sometimes resulting in effortless peak flows. What we require for such events is to neither be so nervous that we are stiff, nor completely relaxed. Again, you might think of the kind of form an athlete must be in—energized, poised, with optimal body use.

Chapter Eight includes several relaxation exercises. Some are described in detail; others are scripts for you to read into a recording device and then use with eyes closed, or ask a friend to read to you. Before you sign up for lessons or classes in meditative disciplines, you might start with these and see which has the greatest benefit for you. That may guide your choice for further exploration.

Visualization

Most Olympic athletes use visualization, so, for example, an Olympic skier may sit quietly for 15-20 minutes most days of the week and visualize the slope—truly see it in great detail. Then like a movie rolling in her mind, she will see herself ski exactly as she desires, using muscle memory for where she has to shift her weight, bend her knees, and so on. She is, in essence, programming herself for success. Musicians can do the same! In his mind's eye, a clarinetist could watch himself walk onstage, bow, adjust the music stand, adjust the reed (these kinds of details help the visualization to take on a real-life quality and help the mind to latch onto the visualization) and then play exactly as he would like it to sound—remembering where he needs to think about fingering or tonguing, all the various dynamics and beauty of tone. It is important to hear the music in real time and not rush through. If the upcoming performance is an audition and you do not know what the hall looks like, pull your range in a bit and focus on your body and clothing.

If you have had a peak performance—one in which everything seemed to flow, or just a very good outing, take a few minutes and remember it. Close your eyes, hear the music in real time, and see if you can "remember" that experience. Your remembrance may be beyond conscious thought—it might feel like body memory or a snippet of a dream or something that is hard to put into words. See if you can re-create the feeling in your body and mind. If there is a recording from that performance, perhaps listening to it will help. Once you have re-experienced that feeling, that balance of heightened energy with poise, attempt to continue that state while shifting to visualizing your new repertoire. You may need to re-capture that state before each movement or piece.

In visualizing repeatedly over days and weeks, you will ease your transition into the Zone when you perform. In every practice or rehearsal, take what singers call a "prep": looking down at the ground or at your feet, breathing deeply, use a few moments before you sing or play to hear the music exactly the way you want it to sound. When you raise your head, the accompanist will know to begin without your having to nod or do any other indication. Using a prep can also serve as a mental "curtain" for the audience—allowing them to take in what they have just heard and, just as sherbet cleanses the palate in between gourmet meal courses, the few moments of silence help their minds to clear and to be receptive to the mood of the next movement or song. When you perform, utilizing those few moments to prepare and hear your ideal rendition will help start the flow. You will begin that internal movie and walk right into it—into the beauty and success for which you have programmed yourself.

Affirmations

Another useful tool for ensuring success, affirmations can be done anywhere, anytime. It is best if they are kept secret, as there is something too threatening to the psyche when we share such inner-reconstruction material with others. It is also important to frame the affirmation in a positive way. If you say, "When I perform, I will not be nervous" the unconscious, which is very literal, hears "nervous" without the "not." It is also vital to state your affirmation as an already established fact. If you say, "When I perform I will be confident" that very literal unconscious mind hears "will" and thinks far into the future. What would be more effective is to affirm something like "Whenever I perform I am grounded and energized and I play (sing) my very best." Repeat it over and over and over. One reason for such repetition is because we are hard wired for fight-or-flight response. The unconscious mind does not differentiate between the threat of a performance and the threat of a wild animal. The fear is real and strong! Yet, if we calm ourselves over and over and prepare ourselves to focus and to succeed, the overwhelming fear becomes more akin to excitement—a very manageable amount of arousal.

Many people find it helpful to tie their affirmation to a regular habit—perhaps keeping a card with affirmations next to the toothbrush. You could also keep them in a pocket or wallet and when waiting in line at the bank or store repeat them silently to yourself. Driving is a good time to repeat affirmations as the monotony of the task can lull us into a slightly meditative state and allow the re-programming of affirmations to go even deeper. Another aid to effective self-programming is to breathe deeply with your affirmation and repeat it in a very regular rhythm. You might even set your affirmation to music and mentally sing it. It can also be helpful to repeat affirmations while walking or biking or doing other forms of exercise. The movement and the accompanying deep breathing tend to help the "re-programming" go even deeper.

If you find in visualizing or in repeating affirmations that some fear pops up:

1. Acknowledge it—do not push it down in your effort to stay with the task at hand.

2. Try to determine the nature of the fear. Is it something tangible, such as "Oh, I really don't have that last page memorized fully!" or "Those runs in the third movement are still beyond me!" – Then there is something you can do, clearly: work on the memorization or the runs.

3. If it is free-floating anxiety such as "Who the heck do I think I am?" "I can't do this" "I'm no good" and so forth, try having a dialogue with that voice. You might need to pump yourself up with energy and power first (see the Flame Exercise in Chapter Six). Say to that inner voice that if it has some specific thing to tell you, to help you, fine. Otherwise, you are not having any of this nonsense today! (For a much more thorough dialogue exercise, see the Jungian Active Imagination in Chapter Six).

4. Take several deep breaths and go back to your affirmation or visualization.

Chapter Three

PRACTICING

"May the light of your soul bless your work with love and warmth of heart."--John O'Donohue

No amount of tips, hints or mental techniques can substitute for regular, thorough practice and knowing the score as well as if you had written it yourself. A solid base of technique combined with technical and interpretive mastery of the music will go a long way towards providing confidence and allaying fears.

A recent book by Geoff Colvin, *Talent is Overrated*, gives many examples of artists, scientists and athletes commonly considered to be geniuses or exceptionally gifted, and describes how in each case, the individual had early, consistent support and training along with hours and hours of work at their specialty. One example is Jerry Rice, often considered the greatest receiver in National Football League history, who devised a training regimen for himself that would cover for every possible pitfall or problem. It was so demanding that his coaches would not describe it to the public for fear that other athletes, copying the regimen, would suffer permanent injury!

The need for practice, preparation and study flies in the face of contemporary culture's lust for instant gratification.

Along with the benefits of the cyber age, such as greater connection, global awareness and access to information, comes an increasing impatience with anything that takes time, work and patience fueled by our acclimation to instantaneous results from computers and handheld devices. This is further compounded by television programs that (falsely) portray achievement in dancing, singing, and other performance modes as something attained very quickly, with just a few coaching sessions or tips. Their depictions of success usually include the notion of immediate celebrity status, including wealth, fame and recording contracts.   If you take the time to read comprehensive interviews or biographies of the best singers and actors, you will find that their success is built on hard work and discipline, not some intangible talent or ability that magically erases any stage fright.

Yet, at workshops on overcoming performance anxiety, I often see crestfallen faces when I reveal that there is no "silver bullet", no **one** answer to ensure self-assurance and poise. Those same faces are filled with surprise when I describe the kind of work necessary to attain confidence in performing. Just as musicians need to practice performance anxiety techniques along with their music, they also need simply to work! The question, however, is not the number of hours. Simply logging time in the practice studio or in one's living room, doing the same things over and over without planning and thought will offer little result. Practicing effectively, however, will reap great rewards.

1. Practice when you are fresh and alert—preferably late morning or early afternoon. If practicing follows a full academic or working day, take a brisk walk first or do something else that will both help you shake off cares and worries and tension, and also give you energy.

2. Do some gentle stretches beforehand. For singers, the body is the instrument and for instrumentalists, the body is at least an equal partner to the instrument— they need to be "tuned" and rid of as much tension as possible.

3. Singers often eat a light meal or snack before singing, as the chewing and swallowing help warm-up the same muscles used for singing.

4. Warm up slowly and carefully, looking for the correct coordination rather than a beautiful sound. Be patient and come back to practicing later if playing or singing does not feel energized and loose.

5. Avoid over-practicing. I am often shocked at the number of hours young people practice—eluding injury only because of their youth. Beginning singers should not practice more than an hour at a time, building up slowly as their technique and stamina improve. Instrumentalists could possibly do two or three hours—but be sure to check with your teacher and watch for any inkling of discomfort or strain. **It's best for all musicians to break up practicing into smaller segments**, if possible. Also mental practicing and score study often prepare you more fully and save wear and tear on your body.

The described regimen of the NFL receiver indicated how he practiced certain runs or calisthenics for particular challenges in the game. We can work similarly. Find the spots in your pieces that trouble you the most and, after a thorough warm-up, address them <u>first</u>. When we have tricky runs or difficult shifts or places that feel too high vocally, we tend to avoid them. Embrace them, instead! Ask your teachers and coaches about ways to make the problem spots easier. Here are a few general ideas:

**For tricky runs, hard rhythms, or awkward leaps:

- Work backwards. Play the last two notes three times, and then add a note or two before and play that combination three times, keep adding until you have the whole passage.

- Then play it forwards, but vary the rhythms: dotting different notes, grouping some into triplets.

- Try it all staccato, then all legato.

- Vary the dynamics: start piano and grow to forte, then reverse. Try starting softly, building to forte in the middle of the phrase, and then tapering off again at the end. The reverse works well, also.

- Then put it away for a day and usually the unconscious mind continues to "work" on it and when next attempted, it is much easier.

For singers, if you need to do such work, try it on a lip-trill, as you are much less likely to tense or feel strain. If lip-trills are difficult to sustain, you can try humming into a straw, or a very hollow hum as if closing around an "OH" vowel so that the molars in the back do not meet, or try an open mouth hum—open the mouth in an "OH" shape with a relaxed jaw and cover your lips with the palm of your hand to hum.

**Start with the last page or pages of your piece.*

We usually start at the beginning, so the first parts of movements or songs feel comfortable. Get muscle memory to work for you by making the latter parts comfortable and well known. A typical practice session of 20 minutes (after you have warmed up) might include working on the last pages of three songs or pieces and then singing or playing just one all the way through.

**Strategize your session:*

An article going around the internet by Dr. Christine Carter demonstrates how we are hard-wired to pay attention to change, but to ignore repetition. For that reason, it is much more fruitful to practice excerpts—picking a few portions of several pieces and alternating them.

Here is an example aimed at singers. Instrumentalists can easily substitute their own pieces, movements, and études:

Length	Material to Practice
3 minutes	Cadenza from aria A on lip-trill, backwards via note groupings
3 minutes	Different tactics to loosen high notes in song C
3 minutes	Last portion of aria B to work on stamina
3 minutes	Learning rhythms and pitches of song A
3 minutes	Cadenza from aria A on AH down an octave, then at pitch
3 minutes	All of song C

**Practice mindfully:

Mindfully means: tackling the difficult sections first; deciding when you need to play through a work in order to feel the overall structure and pace your energy; occasionally using your session as a sensory, meditative time; and performing during the practice time, especially when approaching a concert. Be sure to include some rewards such as playing through old favorites at the end of a session or singing something just for fun.

**Use optimum concentration and focus:

If your schedule allows, it is far more fruitful to have two or three shorter practice periods in a day than one long one for reasons of fatigue and optimum mental retention. In essence, both singers and instrumentalists are engaging in motor skill training, which most of us stop after our earliest years. Allowing the body and mind time to absorb what you have just worked on is especially helpful. Another ramification of the motor skill aspect is replication. If you play or sing a passage successfully for the first time, immediately repeat it! Some specialists in learning theory say that we only have <u>four seconds</u> to get that patterning imprinted in our brains.

**Treat yourself to a silly rehearsal:

While it is important to spend concentrated, quality time on musical challenges and structure your practicing for greatest effect, it is also very helpful to use your imagination and sense of humor in working on your music and your performing abilities. Having an occasional "zany" session can free up expression, allow for creative approaches to technical challenges, and help us "own" the pieces we sing or play. I do not suggest that you do silly things just to liven up your practice or as a cure for boredom. The reason to have a few wacky sessions is to unleash your creativity. The noted Jungian psychoanalyst, author, and lecturer, Dr. Clarissa Pinkola Estés explains in her recording *The Creative Fire* (*) that one of the best ways to get "unstuck" --from a writer's block, from an artist's loss of direction or from being "stale" in performance-- is to use humor. In fact, she suggests that the creative path <u>requires</u> approaching our music or writing or dance with a great deal of playfulness, a sense of enjoying the journey without a goal in sight. So give yourself some practice or rehearsal times to play or sing with some screwball approaches:

> ➢ Sing or play your piece in an opposite style. If you are working on a musical theatre song, sing it as if it were from a Baroque Oratorio or Romantic Era Grand Opera. If it is a Bach concerto, play it as if it were Rachmaninoff, and vice versa. If it is opera, try it in a pop or country-western style. A trio from the Classical era would find new riches if played in rock or bluegrass style!

> ➢ For singers: stage the piece—even if it is a simple art song. Use costumes, props, friends who react to what you sing. Turn your song into a melodrama—exaggerate it, mock it, make it campy.

➤ If you have an accompanist who is willing, it can be especially fruitful for your sense of ensemble and the flow of creativity to practice your piece in a wooden, strict, metronomic way. Next perform it as hammy, schmaltzy, and over-the-top as you can. In the last repetition, let the piece or song play or sing itself—get yourself "out of the way", allow it to emerge. Then reflect with each other on the three versions. You will likely find many new treasures of interpretation.

➤ For singers, try your piece in a variety of poses and postures: kneeling, arms raised in conquest, arms open in contrition, and so forth. Alternate using stances that complement the mood or the character's motivation with those that are opposite.

➤ Play or sing your piece with a variety of feelings— perhaps use flashcards with very strong emotions (rage, lust, vengeance, terror). Pull out a card and sing or play the next phrase that way. Some emotions may work better than others on various days.

➤ Sing or play your piece in the opposite mood than logic would dictate. If it is a piece or tale of mourning, sing or play it as if full of infectious, bubbly joy.

➤ For singers, perform your aria in an opposite character. If you are a maid imploring for understanding, sing it as if you were the queen.

➤ For singers, if your song is in a foreign language, sing it in English. Or sing it in gibberish—aiming for correct expression (which will require that you fully comprehend each written word).

➤ If you have a recording of your piece that you enjoy, put it on and lip-sync or pretend to play while acting the part of a very experienced, confident performer. Then try playing or singing along with the recording.

> For singers, no matter if your piece is a song or an aria, you are likely singing to someone. Can you enlist a friend to be that someone, that "foil?" Seeing their reactions to what you sing can be very helpful in enlivening your own acting and then transferring that energy to times when you sing alone. You might even experiment with asking your "foil" to react in unanticipated, zany ways to what you sing. See what that brings out in your portrayal!

**Use Technology:

Record lessons and coaching sessions and listen at least twice—once with the score, making notes and once without, perhaps with eyes closed, to see for yourself if it is a moving, evocative performance. While it is vital to listen to teachers, coaches and directors, the more we put ourselves "in the driver's seat" the more confident and empowered we feel and that often transfers to confidence onstage.

Ask a friend to make a video of a practice performance. Again, listen once without watching so see if the performance is your most expressive, then watch and determine if you look polished and confident. Singers, this is a great way to check your preparation and judge if your character is believable.

CYCLES OF CREATIVITY

Coming to the practice room on a regular basis is what allows for great creativity. Dr. Estés also explores in *The Creative Fire* the cycles of creativity, so similar to the seasons of the year. Creative life goes through a cycle of birth, rising energy, a zenith, entropy, decline, death, incubation, then again birth and a new cycle. Often when we feel that things are not going well, that we are stale and stuck, we may be in the entropy or death parts of the cycle. While we all need breaks and vacations, it is important to stay with our discipline of practice, no matter where we are in the cycle.

If you are feeling very stuck and stale, perhaps trying some of the zany ideas described above will help, or perhaps a *short* break is needed. The danger is allowing temporary setbacks to keep us from our creative life. If you feel stuck or stale or hollow a great deal of the time, it may be that some deeper psychological work is necessary to restore you to the natural creative cycle.

A QUESTION OF TECHNIQUE

As I mentioned in the first paragraph of this chapter, knowing your music cold and having a solid technique can go a long way towards providing performance confidence. Occasionally, students have said that they suffer from stage fright, when really they were insecure in their technique in all situations. Further discussion would reveal that their discomfort was with them in lessons, in the practice room and even in ensemble rehearsals.

If that is the case for you, please consider some options. It may be that your teacher or parents or peers (or you!) are pushing you into levels of competition and performance for which you are simply not ready. Facing this, discussing the situation and making some changes would be vital.

It also might be possible that you and your teacher are not well matched. This might be manifested in an inability to replicate what is done in a lesson in the practice room. While we all tend to sing and play better in lessons—I'm talking here about consistent lack of progress in practice, meaning that the teacher's ideas and concepts are not jelling in you. Another sign might be your feeling frustrated in lessons and/or your teacher saying that she or he has to repeat herself or himself over and over.

37

Teachers and students commonly build close relationships, so making a studio change can be difficult. If it means better progress, however, it is necessary.

MEMORIZING

Part of practicing and preparing to perform involves memorization. In my experience, folks who sight read well often have trouble with memorizing and vice versa. Yet there is a tendency to make the task harder than it really is—in street parlance, to "psych yourself out." Frequently college students will complain that they have an inordinately difficult time memorizing, yet these same students are successful memorizing for other classes. Almost all study involves memorization of facts, data, periodic tables, sequences and so forth. I truly believe the problem with music memorization is that people do not give it the kind of concentrated effort applied to other studies. Some people memorize easily, but for most it takes hours of study, repetition and coming at the process from several vantage points.

If memorizing is a challenge for you, take heart: below are some strategies to try.

- ✓ Study your scores frequently. Analyze the relationship of solo line to accompaniment. Who is soloist when? Does the accompaniment follow the mood of the solo line or anticipate a mood change? What part of the inner life of the work is expressed by the accompaniment?

- ✓ Singers: study the relationship of text to music. Does your line or the accompaniment word-paint or underscore dramatic moments in the text? What is the composer's interpretation of the text?

- ✓ Do a harmonic analysis of the score. Often seeing the harmonic rhythm and the overall harmonic structure of the piece can help the mind grasp how the piece unfolds.

✓ For singers: draw pictures of the unfolding of the story. Instrumentalists: invent a story for your piece and do the same.

✓ If possible, act out the story in melodrama or pantomime.

✓ Play or sing a few measures or phrases several times, then put down the score and repeat from memory.

✓ In long works, select certain measures or phrases as your "anchors"—work especially on memorizing these (which may require drilling measures over and over) so that if you get a bit lost and need to "jump"—you may.

✓ For singers: write out your texts and carry them with you. Try memorizing a few lines while waiting in line at the bank or store. Memorize as you drive—the quasi-meditative state induced by driving can help with memorization.

✓ Listen over and over to a recording of yourself playing or singing. When we listen to others, especially professional recordings, part of our brain shuts down in the belief that we are being entertained—so we concentrate less effectively.

✓ Get the piece IN your body by doing some of the conducting, dancing, and bowing described in Chapter Four.

✓ Some people find it helpful to use physical movement of various forms while thinking through the phrases or texts. Using gestures, making faces, walking, running, hopping, bending, stretching, making signals with the arms—all can be helpful to musicians in general and those who learn kinesthetically in particular.

✓ Although some people memorize easily, for many others it takes hours of time. Plan for that and prepare in advance.

CHARACTER PREPARATION

Singers, your work on character preparation for your songs and arias is the foundation for focus in performing, as described in Chapter Two. Consider it a vital part of your practice and performance preparation.

If your schedule allows, take some straight acting classes. Learning the craft of acting away from all the attention singing requires can be very helpful. Working on a variety of scenes and monologues can help you discover how to "put on" a character quickly and effectively.

✳ For operas or musical theatre plays, research the era in which it is set. If it is based on a book or play, read the original as it will no doubt give you greater understanding of the story and deeper insights into your character. Watch videos of other plays set in that time. Think of yourself as a cultural anthropologist, attempting to understand what makes individuals "tick" and societies work.

✳ Read through the libretto, discovering what others say about your character and what the character says about himself or herself. What does the character's language (direct, blunt, flowery, poetic, obtuse) say about her or him? What does the character's music (lofting, dramatic, sweet, halting, highly decorated) say about him or her? What does the orchestration (light, full, use of leitmotifs, use of certain instruments or combinations of instruments when the character sings) say about her or him?

✳ Take 20-30 minutes to sketch out a full characterization for every aria and song in your repertoire. Specificity is vital to effective acting! Make concrete, specific choices—you can always make changes later on. Answer at least these questions:

1. Who am I? (Age, status, family, pet peeves, fears, vocation, favorite color, secrets, dreams and goals, appearance, hobbies, past loves, etc.)

2. Where am I? (Indoors or out, room, area of room—describe in detail)

3. What time is it? (year, season, time of day)

4. What just happened before I began to sing?

5. What is my motivation (what I want) and obstacle (what is in the way)? Note: there is always a motivation and an obstacle. If they are not readily apparent, spend some time thinking about them. Even if it is a love song and all seems rosy, there is always a chance of losing the lover or dying.

6. To whom am I singing? How do I want him/her/them to react?

7. What happens when I finish singing?

   ** *At the end of this chapter is a form that you can photocopy and use to do your character work.* **

Here are a student's replies to those questions about *The Rovin' Gambler,* a folk poem that has been set in a variety of ways. The composer, John Jacob Niles, set it to a simple folk-like melody that is repeated for all the verses. Because the melody is quite simple, the student focused on the text for his analysis. (With thanks to former student, Edek Sher).

I am a rovin' gambler; I've been in many a town.
Where're I see a pack of cards I lay my money down,
I lay my money down.
With a click clack oh and a high Johnny ho,
I lay my money down.

I hadn't been a packet man many more weeks than three
When I fell in love with a St. Louis girl and she in love with me,
And she in love with me.
With a click clack oh and a high Johnny ho
And she in love with me.

We went in the back parlor, she cooled me with her fan,
And she whispered soft in her mother's ear,
"I love my gamblin' man, I love my gamblin' man.
With a click clack oh and a high Johnny ho
I love my gamblin' man.

"Oh daughter dear, dear daughter, how could you do me so?
To leave your dear old mother and with this gambler go,
And with this gambler go?
With a click clack oh and a high Johnny ho,
And with this gambler go?"

"'Tis true I love you dearly, 'Tis true I love you well,
But the love I have for the gamblin' man no human tongue can tell,
No human tongue can tell.
With a click clack oh and a high Johnny ho,
No human tongue can tell."

She picked up her satchel and she did leave her home,
And on the steamer "Morning Star" the two of them did roam,
The two of them did roam.
With a click clack oh and a high Johnny ho,
The two of them did roam.

1. *Who am I?* I am a strapping young lad, 25 years old. I have an addiction to gambling, which influences every decision I make. For example, just a fortnight ago I got into a fight with a child over a halfpenny I saw lying on the ground. The little brat said that it was his and he had dropped it only moments before I spotted it from across the way and knocked over two elderly ladies, a cart of carrots and a tomato stand in my pursuit of the coin. I was taken to the station by an officer and had to pay a penny to get out. This happens a lot. I have no family; they have made sure of this. I am not allowed within a half-mile of their lodgings.

2. *Where am I?* I am all over the place! While I spend most of my time in dank bars that reek of smoke and rat excrement, I get out just enough to beg for money and meet women whom I only pursue for their purse-strings.

3. *What time is it?* It is fall, as can be seen by the hat my last woman knit for me out of her love for me. I am so smooth and cunning that I can make a girl fall in love with me in the course of three hours, which is what I do here. It starts at 11:00 a.m. when I am in St. Louis and ends at 2:00 p.m. when we board a steamer together. She should have listened to her mother.

4. *What just happened before I began to sing?* I was lamenting the loss of my love (while in a gutter), or rather the money that the girl who loved me had. She was the daughter of a baron and had so much money! I was in a bad state because I was out of money and saw cards being thrown down all about me. This is when I met my sweet lady, Isabelle. She got me out of the dumps (literally) and I promised her a life of adventure.

5. *What is my motivation?* As I have said, I want money so I can gamble, smoke and drink. But I don't get paid much as a packet man.

6. *To whom am I singing?* I am singing to the men on the steamer in a musty bar. I am drunk and while I am normally modest about my adventures, I can't control myself.

7. *What happens when I finish singing?* After we run away together and board the steamer, it is all fun and games! It turns out that Isabelle loves gambling, too, and she can counterfeit money without flaw. And while I like to

think that I duped her into falling in love with me, I feel that the tables are turned sometimes. I hope she doesn't treat me the way I have treated all my previous women.

Notice all the details in the answers and how Edek created a believable, interesting character—one that almost jumps off the page. Specificity is the actor's friend—creating a quirk or a character-betraying gesture or a personality flaw can help make the character real to you and to the audience.

(*) Estés, Clarissa Pinkola. *The Creative Fire*. Boulder, CO: Sounds True, 2005. CD.

--Character Analysis Form on the following page.--

CHARACTER ANALYSIS FORM
(Remember: specificity is the actor's best tool!)

Title of song/aria: _____

Who am I? (Status: high=royalty, low=servant; Age;
Relationships: do I have family, am I in a love relationship)

If I could tell you three things I love, three things I fear,
three things I hope for, three things I dread, and three things
I dislike, they would be:

What time is it? (Season of year; Time of day; Era of
history)

Where am I? (Outdoors, inside, room, area) Describe in detail:

What just happened?

What is my motivation (what I want) and obstacle (what is in the way)? If the piece is from a play or an opera, what is my through-line (over-all motivation in the show)?

To whom am I singing? How do I want him/her to respond?

What happens next?

What does my language (flowery, direct, blunt, etc.) and music (sweet, dramatic, sensuous) say about me?

If the piece is from a play or an opera, what do the other characters say about me? Any suggestions for gestures, change of focus, and so forth from the orchestra?

Chapter Four

PERFORMANCE PREPARATION

"The public comes to the theatre not because they want to heckle and see things go wrong. They come because they hope it's going to be wonderful, and they're going to join in that one special occasion, that special night." – Ingrid Bergman

Musicians put in countless hours of practice, focusing on correct notes and rhythms, legato and beauty of tone. Simply maintaining some instruments and preparing reeds or strings or bows takes a great deal of effort and singers need to spend time on diction, bodywork and awareness, character development, and acting as well. Yet how often do we practice performing? It is a curious phenomenon. You would not expect a runner to be successful at a marathon without prior preparation. Runners start, of course, with training, followed by participating in short races, learning from that experience, perhaps changing some training aspects, then continuing with longer and longer runs, building on those successes and finally attempting their first marathon. Yet musicians so often throw themselves (or allow themselves to be recruited for) *important* performances without taking the necessary *small* steps first. Frequently new voice students tell me that they suffer from performance anxiety and when asked how often they perform, reply, "Oh, it's really been years. So when I tried last month, it was just awful!" Now you would not expect a baseball pitcher who had taken a couple years off, to suddenly get in and pitch a perfect game! One of the things that can make for performance jitters is such an unrealistic expectation.

Ideally, musicians begin with smaller outings, gradually increasing in importance and visibility, just as runners go from short sprints to marathons. Starting with performing one song or piece in an informal studio class and repeating this several times, moving to larger gatherings of musicians –usually called convocations or collegiums or departmental recitals in academic settings. The next step is often opera or music theatre chorus for singers and chamber group or small orchestra or wind ensemble for instrumentalists. A shared recital with another musician is frequently next, followed by a solo recital or soloist for a concerto or an opera rôle. Certainly each of these "steps" could (and ideally should) be repeated several times. In addition to step-wise performances, below are some activities that will prepare you to perform:

※ Record your rehearsals and listen at least twice: once with the score, making notes for yourself regarding technical and interpretive matters and once without the score, perhaps with your eyes closed, determining if it is the kind of evocative performance you desire. While the advice of teachers and coaches is valuable, to be respected and heeded, it can also be very empowering to make your own interpretive decisions, allowing you to feel "in the driver's seat"—more in charge. Feeling more "in charge" can help boost confidence when performing.

※ Make videos of rehearsals and listen once without watching to evaluate, again, if it is the kind of performance you desire. Then watch and see if your entrances, exits, bows and the performance itself look polished, graceful and professional. In that regard, videos can be highly effective teachers! While viewing, singers might want to turn the volume all the way down to determine if the physical acting is effective on its own.

✳ On occasion, listen to a recording of yourself singing or playing (perhaps from your last rehearsal) and simply mime the performing, with the goal of practicing the performance elements—the professional posture and walk, the bows, the visual focus, and, for singers, all the acting aspects. THIS IS IMPORTANT and a step that is often overlooked. Practicing the performance elements will go a long way towards building performance confidence.

✳ Keep a practice and rehearsal log. (You might combine it with the performance log discussed in Chapter Five.) Note the amount of time practiced or rehearsed, at what time of day, under what kinds of conditions, as this can help you plan for the most efficient rehearsing. If you jot down insights and breakthroughs as well as problems and questions, share them with your teachers and coaches at the beginning of your next sessions—to help determine the focus or direction of that lesson or coaching. Use some journal time to devise short and long-term goals for yourself—especially for each performance. Perhaps for one outing you simply want to take deeper breaths or be more aware of your breathing in general. Coming up with one technical goal and one interpretive goal for each performance is enough! Adding more and more goals over time will eventually lead to artistry. Setting short and long term goals can also assist in attaining that laboratory-approach, healthy detachment that helps you view each performance as only one in a series.

BRAIN ACTIVITY AND PERFORMING

When a musician is stimulated, excited, nervous the left hemisphere, more closely tied with language and logical thought, shuts down to some degree. That can be beneficial, as

50

the right hemisphere takes over. It is associated with images, sensations, the arts, and is connected to the Parasympathetic Nervous Response, which, despite its name, calms us down. However, since the left hemisphere is less active, it is vital to be memorized early. When performing, you cannot count on the left hemisphere helping you to remember words and music. In fact, being so well memorized that you can, in essence, go on automatic pilot, builds confidence in itself. I ask my students to be memorized six weeks in advance and we actually do a memory check in which they perform for friends, other students, and/or teachers to determine, *in performance mode*, if the material is fully memorized. Truly memorized means secure of part with or without accompaniment, and the performance is musically, textually -for singers-, stylistically and expressively secure and convincing.

From the memory check onward, I ask students to perform the music in lessons, even if we start and stop and work on technical matters, because practicing performing helps to trigger the right hemisphere to be fully engaged (it also helps one to get into performance mode—please see Chapter Six).

MORE TRIGGERS FOR THE RIGHT BRAIN

- Sensory practice: imagine that your whole body is playing or singing –it can help to close your eyes. On a regular basis, use part of a practice session or rehearsal to simply savor the music and tune into the sensations involved in producing it. See if you can recapture the initial attraction that led you to perform this particular piece or the excitement that led you to studying this particular instrument.

- If you are a singer or a wind player, imagine that you breathe through the soles of your feet and your whole body acts as a conduit for air and tone. Some people find it helpful to imagine that upon inhalation, their whole body fills up with air and as they play or sing, the air and tone go up the back of the body and over the head. If you are a pianist or string player, imagine that your body amplifies the sound along with your instrument.

- Hear your piece in real time, do not rush through, and conduct an imaginary performer singing or playing it. If you are unfamiliar with conducting patterns, simply wave your arms to the flow of the music. This can be a great memory check as well: you will not be able to conduct passages that are not completely memorized. Another time, bow an imaginary cello or violin (string players might try singing or pretending to play another instrument). Perhaps the most effective technique is to let the sweep of the music take you in a free form dance – do not think it through or plan it. These activities not only help engage the right hemisphere, but are also a wonderful way to practice on days that your voice or lip is tired or you are a little under the weather.

- Hear your piece and conduct, or bow or dance as just described, but do just a portion of the music and then immediately go back and play or sing it. This allows for a great transfer of energy, vibrancy and legato. It is also an effective tool for getting the piece "in" your body, your fingers, your mind, and helping you to truly own it.

- In preparing for a recital, keep a list of all the important technical and interpretive points for each piece. As you study your scores, bear these points in mind and, as you practice, you will solve more and more of them. When you are about 10 days away from the event, pare your list down to the one most important technical point and the single most vital interpretive aspect for each piece or movement, because, in addition to the areas of focus mentioned in Chapter Two, most people can only think of two things while performing. You can even memorize this list of points and when taking a few seconds of preparation, be thinking them. To engage the right hemisphere more fully, come up with images or sensations instead. If the most important technical aspect of a given song is to support, it would engage the right hemisphere to think, "What would it feel like to keep up a loose belt while I sing?" and if the most vital interpretive aspect is a regal bearing, the right hemisphere would be triggered when visualizing a king or queen.

- Study your scores. Hear the music in real time, do not rush through, and, for singers and wind players, breathe where you would really breathe –attempting to remember the sensations of playing or singing the piece as you go along. Hear yourself play or sing exactly as you would like it to sound and, at the same time, follow along in your score, noting all the markings you have made and remembering the technical aspects. In that way, you are utilizing and coordinating both hemispheres and programming yourself for success. You might find it valuable, in the few days prior to a performance, to play or sing just enough to keep in shape, and spend most of your regular practice time doing this kind of activity.

PREPARE YOURSELF FOR SUCCESS AND COMFORT

It is vital to practice every aspect of performing: how you walk on stage, acknowledge other participants, bow, and so forth. In concert or recital, we do what we have rehearsed, and practicing all these elements will mean that nothing can surprise you or catch you off guard.

For example, several years ago I was singing in the choir at the Cathedral of Saint John the Divine in New York City. We were about to process down the aisle and sing an Evensong service for which we had rehearsed the music, but never practiced the processing or holding folders and candles or any other aspect. For her own musical enjoyment, the actress Linda Lavin was singing with us and I was her processing partner that evening. This was a woman who had had a major television

53

series in the 1970s along with a rewarding theatrical career, including having just won a Tony award for her rôle in the play, *Broadway Bound.* Yet she touched my arm with an ice-cold hand and said, "I'm so scared, I'm about to throw up!" Why? Because despite all her experiences on stage, this was a new venue and she was out of her comfort zone. Had we practiced all the mechanics of lining up and processing and holding our folders with candles and singing—I am certain it would have been far less frightening to her. If such a seasoned performer can be thrown off by lack of rehearsal, imagine the ramifications for those just starting out!

Think of sporting events such as games or competitions like the Olympics. Can you envision visiting baseball teams having no chance to try out the field, or a skier competing without at least one practice session on the slope? Again, as musicians, students often put unreasonable expectations on themselves that athletes and professional musicians would never do.

Another way to think of preparing is to imagine a family moving from one side of town to the other. The youngest child is afraid because it is new, unknown, and, therefore, scary. So the loving parent or older sibling will take the child to the new home and explore it, play some games, have a meal, walk around the neighborhood, perhaps have a sleep over. Suddenly what was unknown is now known and far less fearsome. Musicians can also make what is unknown and frightening known and much less threatening—here are some ways:

✓ **Practice in the performance space**! Professional musicians' contracts often specify a certain number of hours of rehearsal time in the concert or recital hall, so it puzzles me why students and aspiring professionals often think they can skip this important step. It is an opportunity to be gentle with yourself and your colleagues in acclimating to the space and checking the acoustics. Once again, it makes the unfamiliar known and more comfortable. Often performance spaces in academic settings are heavily booked, but at least inquire, and do everything in your power to get as much time in there as possible. Can your teacher or coach reserve some time or advocate for you? Can you and your accompanist be flexible and rehearse late at night or early in the morning or some other open time?

✓ **Practice for several weeks in your performance outfit.** That way, you have plenty of opportunities to discover if your suit coat will allow for effective bowing, or your gown has enough room for deep breathing and support. Pay particular attention to your shoes. Do they help you feel grounded and rooted? If not, get yourself another pair! (Most women like to have some amount of heel— but avoid stilettos and heels greater than 2 inches or so.) Be sure that any clothes chosen for performing and auditioning are kept only for that purpose. That way you avoid any last-minute panic, such as discovering rips or food stains. Keeping performance clothes free from everyday use and practicing frequently in them helps in a subtle psychological way, as it turns your outfit into your uniform. When I was in graduate school my voice teacher, Dr. Bruce Kolb, said to me: "Some people put on a suit and tie and they go to work. Others put on a custodian's outfit or a nurse's uniform, and they go to work. You put on your audition clothes, and you go to work!" It is a subtle mental shift. I still did the best I could do; I still gave it my all. But by thinking of auditioning and performing as simply doing my job, I felt much less pressure: I need not give the performance of my life; I did not have to prove myself or even get the gig. I simply did my job. Maintaining audition and performance clothes only for those purposes can be an effective tool to assist in getting in that frame of mind: you put on your "uniform" and you are ready to go to work.

✓ **Practice your entrances, your exits, and your bows— leave nothing to chance!** Once again, this is something that most professionals insist on, so please do not avoid this necessary part of rehearsal. It is yet another way to

✓ **Recruit a stage manager.** Particularly if you are giving a recital or concert with several colleagues, it would be wise to recruit a musician friend to set up the stage. This person can arrange the various chairs, stands and even take the scores onstage so that players need only bring their instruments. If appropriate to the hall, the stage manager can also raise and dim lights. Sometimes they give introductory remarks: reminding the audience to turn program pages quietly, reserve applause for breaks after groups or entire works, silence cell phones and refrain from texting during the performance. The stage manager can also announce the intermission and its length and occasionally, this person will also serve as page-turner. Whatever duties you would like her or him to take, communicate them well in advance, along with a program that has clear instructions about how each work or group is to be set up. Stage-managing can be a great favor from a colleague and one that is easy to return.

✓ **Practice your music; taking breaks no longer than you will take in the actual performance.** This will help you in pacing yourself, feeling the flow of the music and the energy, and allowing yourself to get into concert mode. Instead of relying on just one dress rehearsal to discover those things, give yourself several opportunities to practice the overall sweep of your performance. If you know well in advance what time of day your outing will be, attempt to rehearse at the same time. If you are assigned, say, 4:00 in the afternoon and that is usually a low-energy time for you, rehearsing at that time can supply you with opportunities to discover how to prepare for the performance—perhaps a nap a few hours prior or eating the right amount of protein and carbohydrates in the morning. Be sure to practice truly performing, not stopping for mistakes or indicating that they have happened. We do in performance what we have practiced, so practice recovering from mistakes, looking for and releasing tension, and using a mantra to get back in the flow.

✓ **Schedule out- of- town or mini performances.** Professional musicians regularly give out-of-town performances first before they try new material or new venues. Students and aspiring professionals can do the same. If you are in school, can you give part or your entire recital at home during semester break? Or perhaps your teacher will allow you to use some lesson time to perform for friends. Maybe you have relatives in town who would relish hearing part of your program in their living room? Are you a member of a church or synagogue that would enjoy hearing a song or a movement of a piece as a voluntary? One prevalent fallacy among musicians is the idea of "peaking" too soon—that is very rare. Think of professionals who play some compositions over and over, finding new levels of expression each time. It is highly unlikely that giving some extra pre-concert performances will make you stale. On the contrary, they will most likely help you feel more confident and give your interpretation new depths.

✓ **Schedule your dress rehearsal at least four days in advance, if possible.** That way you have time to learn from the rehearsal, to listen to a recording or watch a video from the rehearsal and absorb that information. And if there are a FEW minor changes, it is possible to make them. One recipe for creating performance anxiety is to make a lot of last-minute changes. While one new insight from your teacher or your own study may help give the performance extra sparkle, a lot of new ideas and insights, new approaches or rearranging things simply throws you off center and negates the careful preparation you have done. However, if your dress rehearsal is far enough in advance, it may be possible to make those very few alterations without disrupting the overall structure of your program and the energy flow you have established.

SOME THOUGHTS ABOUT MISTAKES

Frequently students will confess in workshops that their greatest fear, and focus, in performing is making a mistake. Like a singer overly concerned with the possibility of phlegm, that kind of worry –with the attendant constriction of muscles and energy—will make the dreaded outcome all the more likely!

TIP: The audience will forgive mistakes!

I repeat, the audience <u>will</u> forgive mistakes, but will <u>not</u> forgive or forget if the musician allows the fear of making errors to rob their performance of vibrancy, emotion and communication. Remember the quote from Ms. Von Stade in Chapter Two? Listeners want to hear stories (whether actual or abstract) and be moved! Our job, as performers, is to tell those stories. It is that simple and that profound. By obsessing over mistakes, we move our efforts away from giving the audience that experience of emotional catharsis and transcendence to directing the energy inward. The spectators will feel cheated, for certain.

By and large, audiences are very much on the musician's side. Frequently college-aged students find this hard to believe. That is partly due to one emphasis of undergraduate education: developing a keen sense of analysis, discrimination, and critical thinking. During the development of those capabilities, students are habitually very judgmental of themselves and others, indeed. However, as one continues to grow and mature, especially through the difficulties that life can present, critical thinking is usually matched with greater empathy and acceptance.

Listeners from the general population, however, are very much in the performer's corner. You can feel them relax, sit back and savor concerts when the musician is self-assured. One reason for playing the rôle of an experienced, confident artiste is to set the audience's minds at ease. As mentioned before, the more you play the part of a seasoned professional, the more truly confident you will feel.

The performance anxiety expert, Don Greene, was interviewed some time ago on CBS television's *The Early Show*. He discussed recovering from mistakes, in steps:

1. Accept that the mistake happened. Your performance will not be flawless, and move on!

2. If you hear an inner critical voice, tell it to shut up! It is NOT the voice of God! You do not have time while performing to listen.

3. Look for body tension (we usually tense in some way when we err) and release it.

4. Use a mantra, an affirmation you have prepared, to get back in the flow.

Mind you, all this needs to happen within seconds, even nano-seconds, hence the need to be prepared. Therefore, practice in performance mode without stopping for mistakes, or indicating that they have happened, seeking out tension and releasing it. If you are the kind of performer who hears inner critical voices, try the Jungian Active Imagination exercise in Chapter Eight or the exercise on confronting your inner judges in Eloise Ristad's book, *A Soprano on Her Head*. Freeing yourself of this constant loop of inner criticism is essential. However, in performance, as Mr. Greene noted, just tell the voice(s) to shut up! Use an affirmation or mantra to get yourself in the zone before you begin each piece or movement and repeat it whenever you make a mistake to resume the flow. (See Chapter Eight for some suggestions.)

It can be beneficial to observe individual athletes compete and notice how forgiving you feel when they err. If a figure skater falls after a jump, the support from the spectators is almost palpable—it is as if they are willing the skater to get back up and continue. The same is true for you! If there is a phlegm ball on your high note or your reed makes a funny sound or your lip gives out on a long phrase—that is the musician's equivalent of falling. The audience does not despise you or think less of you—they want you to get up and get back into it. Do not allow such momentary events to rob them or yourself of the beauty you are creating!

A creative and powerful way to view mistakes or missteps comes from a recent version of Krista Tippett's radio program *On Being*, when the legendary cellist, Yo-Yo Ma, shared his thoughts on performing and audiences and mistakes:

> "While I'm on stage, you're all my guests, because that's sort of the unsaid agreement. So while you're my guests, if something bad happens on stage, I often think of Julia Child. 'Oh! The chicken's fallen on the floor! Oh, well, pick it up and put it right back!' And you know what? *Everybody's* with you. So whatever you practice for . . .it's all right because we have a greater purpose. The greater purpose is that we are communing together and we want this moment to be really special for all of us, because, otherwise, why bother to have come at all? It's not about proving anything! It's about sharing something."

I love this! There is nothing negative or aggressive about it, yet by thinking of yourself as the host or hostess and the audience as guests, it gives you more power. You are in charge; you are setting the scene, rather than feeling like the tiny victim about to enter the lions' den.

His reference to Julia Child, the iconic French Chef, is apt. Her television show was live, not recorded. There was no time to "freak out" if the chicken fell on the floor. So anything that happened had to be okay. Additionally, she was the hostess and we, the viewers, her guests.

So in your rehearsals and performances, channel Julia Child (go watch her on you tube, if you are unfamiliar with her show). Set the scene, welcome your guests. Establish yourself as happily and graciously in charge from the instant you walk onstage. Any mistakes will be "the chicken falling on the floor", which you will put right back and, undisturbed, continue sharing and communing with your audience.

PERFORMANCE PREPARATION AWAY FROM THE PRACTICE ROOM OR CONCERT HALL

It can be valuable to practice performance techniques in other areas of life and in new environments. Once you begin to feel more confident with your mental, physical and performance preparation—start challenging yourself in new ways and in new places, so that even under extreme circumstances, you remain calm and centered.

- Engage in some other competitive, in-the-moment activity. If your schedule allows it and you enjoy fresh challenges, try adding a different kind of activity that makes you focus and learn to achieve in the moment. A student of mine did very well at her first college audition attempts because she already knew how to get in the zone, focus and ignore the competition from years of participating on a swim team. While she still required some ideas from me that were unique to vocal competitions, the swimming experience gave her confidence and maturity that helped a great deal. Sports of all kinds from running races to skating to team sports are helpful as is being part of a debate team or trying your hand at acting or an acting class.

- Organize a peer support group! Especially if you have limited opportunities for informal performances, such as studio classes, talk with some trusted musician friends and schedule a few performance evenings. Let me emphasize the word trusted. At all levels of music-making, there are people who lack the courage to face their own fears and inner "demons," and, instead, aim those negative inner voices outward. This is what causes "diva fits" and undermining others at auditions by asking probing questions or reacting negatively. It is fruitful to learn how to put up mental "armor" and protect yourself from such unscrupulous folks if you are working with them or in school with them. However, do not invite them to your support group. That should, ideally, be a time to attempt novel approaches, fresh ideas, perhaps things that stretch you a bit and make for vulnerability at first, which is best to do within a highly supportive atmosphere. I belonged to such an *ad hoc* peer group when I lived in New York City, made up of singers and accompanists. We would often "report in" on our latest auditions and gigs and network with each other. Held in the evenings, after our day jobs, these performance times were occasionally preceded by a potluck dinner or followed by wine and cheese. We only commented on acting and stagecraft, recognizing that technique was in the hands of the performer and her or his teacher. This is a very effective way to get a lot of performance experience in a short time, with supportive and clarifying feedback.

- How about setting up some exchanges with students from another school or other musicians in a nearby town? Perhaps your teacher or coach can facilitate this, or you might try communicating through student musical organizations such as SNATS or MENC. Arranging for some informal performances, perhaps followed by feedback can simply give everyone more concert experience along with the challenge of applying preparation and centering techniques in a new environment.

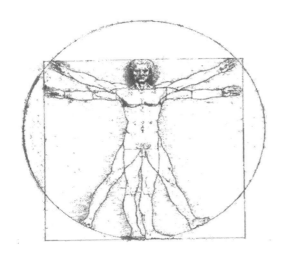

Chapter Five

PHYSICAL PREPARATION

"I was born with music inside me. Music was one of my parts. Like my ribs, my kidneys, my liver, my heart. Like my blood. It was a force already within me when I arrived on the scene. It was a necessity for me--like food or water"-- Ray Charles

It is surprising to many beginning singers how physical good singing technique is: a singer's body IS his or her instrument. Yet an instrumentalist's body should not be ignored, for it certainly can be viewed as an equal partner with the instrument. That is why it is so important to prepare physically for performing.

DAILY DISCIPLINE

One of the realities of a musical career, including training, is discipline. While everyone deserves vacations, time off, and opportunities to "kick up your heels and party"—for performers, a regular partying lifestyle spells doom. In fact, a performing artist is well served by following the kind of regimen that athletes use. You have likely heard these recommendations before:

1. **Get 8 hours or more of sleep each night**! Students often struggle with allowing enough time for sleep, and often "get by" on little rest simply because of their youth. Like youth itself, this will not last! An important part of your undergraduate education is to learn how to plan ahead, make priorities, and focus in your studying so that you are not spinning off from the task and following goat trails—all to have a balanced life and avoid all-nighters and nights of little rest.

   - Sleep is balm for the voice! I can tell a difference in my singing whether I have had, say 7 hours sleep or 10, not only in tone quality but also in scale. After a lot of sleep—I have several more notes at both ends of my range.

   - Sleep is important to instrumentalists in maintaining an inner sense of calm so that fine motor skills are not compromised by nervousness.

   - Several recent studies have indicated that extra sleep helps athletes' performance, strength and endurance. The best results were attained with 10-12 hours of sleep each night! The energy and strength required for musical performance is very similar. In fact, opera singers often report that they actually lose weight during performances, as the body energy required is so great. Oftentimes singers in touring operas will do nothing else but rehearse, perform and sleep—usually aiming for 12 hours.

   - Think of sleep as your foundation for confidence. If your body is well rested you can certainly deal with stressful situations much more easily. By contrast, recall times when you have been sleep deprived:

likely you felt somewhat fragile, easily thrown off center by stressors of all kinds, unable to feel rooted, grounded or centered, and unable to focus.

2. **Exercise on a regular basis.** It seems that the medical community changes its recommendations on a yearly basis, but most medical professionals would suggest at least 30 minutes of cardiovascular exercise 5 to 6 days a week. Some toning and stretches added to that would benefit performers as well. In my experience as a teacher, it appears that more and more students are realizing the benefits of exercise, yet for those who are reluctant to add the discipline to their busy schedules, consider these points:

- Folks who exercise regularly are less likely to catch all the viruses going around. Lower blood pressure and higher energy levels are benefits as well.

- As a singer who suffers from allergies and asthma, I find cardio exercise to be extremely helpful in clearing out my airways. In the past, I would not exercise on performance days, wanting to conserve energy. Now I do at least a brief workout, and plan carefully to allow my body plenty of time to recover. (If you have exercise-induced asthma, consult with your physician regarding how to make cardio exercise a part of your life.) It is especially important to avoid singing for 30-60 minutes after working out, because the vocal folds are in an extreme open position while exercising and the body needs time to relax them before making the kinds of fine adjustments needed in singing.

- You can think of exercise as a natural tranquilizer. Certainly increasing heart rate and respiration helps to discharge stress, rid the body of toxins, and create a sense of well-being by releasing endorphins.

- A combination of cardio exercise and core strengthening can help all people, but especially those who experience nervousness as shaky legs and trembling hands. Feeling as if you are playing or singing from your center can aid in focus and in letting go of extraneous tension. Group Centergy might be ideal, as it combines yoga, pilates with cardio and contributes to core strength. (See Resources section)

- A college student of mine who studied Pilates over the semester is an example of the benefits of toning, stretching and core strengthening. I could hardly believe the great difference in her tone quality, the ease of production and her marvelous posture!

- Meditative movement in disciplines such as Yoga, Tai Chi, and Qi Gong helps unite the body and mind. This can relieve stress and anxiety in daily life and certainly carry over to performing.

- Because singers ARE their instruments and instrumentalists' bodies are certainly equal partners, bodywork of all kinds can be beneficial. Being able to sense and release tension before it becomes chronic, leading to pain and dysfunction, is highly valuable. Bodywork can also assist in the elusive ideal of living IN one's body and in the present. You might explore Nia movement, Feldenkrais Method, Shiatsu or traditional Swedish massage, Rolfing, Yoga, Tai Chi and Qi Gong. The Resources section at the end of this book will give more information.

- Please see chapter ten on the help that Alexander Technique can give, written by my colleague, Diana McCullough. I invited Diana to contribute to this book because I value Alexander Technique so highly. Any of the disciplines or modalities listed above can be highly effective. I personally think that AT is the most valuable because it is something that can be practiced all the time, not just during a one-hour session. It is also an integrative, spiritual approach to being in the moment and in one's body. Those two elements alone can do a great deal to combat performance anxiety.

3. **Your mother was right: eat your vegetables!** You would not expect an engine to perform well, if run by the cheapest fuel available. A diet rich in whole grains and lean protein and veggies will give you the ultimate energy for practicing and performing. The importance of eating fresh produce cannot be overstated—many studies in recent years have shown that they provide not only vitamins but also all manner of trace elements and microscopic components that make for good health. A vitamin supplement can be helpful, but there is no substitute for plenty of fruit and vegetables.

   Take it easy on caffeine and alcohol. Both have an immense effect on the Central Nervous System—obviously something to consider when dealing with nerves. If you drink coffee or tea or caffeinated soda, drink some water alongside, as they are drying to your system. Do the same if you imbibe. (Remaining adequately hydrated is important for overall health, but most especially for singers and wind players.) Along with coffee and tea, sugar is a desiccant! If you use lozenges on a regular basis, get the sugar-free kind. Be aware that menthol can be irritating. Avoid smoking and recreational drugs like the plague!

4. **Take care of your inner life.** Whether you attend worship services of some kind, or meditate or treat yourself to a nice walk or reading some favorite poetry, take time to release stress and to nurture yourself. Students, in particular, often struggle with finding time for their inner lives. Yet, as a friend of mine once said, "When you think you just can't blow something off, that's when you really need to blow it off!" In other

words, when you are so over-scheduled and frazzled that you cannot conceive of creating some time for spirituality or reflection or fun, that is when you need it most.

- Often taking just a half-hour to pray or meditate or enjoy a book or take a walk can refresh you in deep and lasting ways, allowing you to go back to work, studying, or practicing with renewed energy and focus, more than making up for the "lost" 30 minutes.

- Soul Time, as I like to call it, can also help ward off sickness! A former teacher of mine often said, "If you do not take time for yourself, your body will make you do so by becoming ill!" Stress is a big factor in contracting contagious diseases. Consider regular Soul Time as a way to avoid illness and re-charge your mental and creative faculties. (Please see chapter six for more ideas).

PREPARING PHYSICALLY FOR A PERFORMANCE

Two or Three Weeks Ahead

In the last few weeks before a big event, such as a solo recital, playing a concerto with orchestra, or a rôle in opera or oratorio, treat yourself as if you were preparing for a marathon. If at all possible, get some extra sleep, especially in the week before the performance. You may be too excited to sleep much the night before and you can, in essence, draw on this "bank of rest." Eat nourishing, easily digested food, hydrate, exercise regularly and, if possible, increase your Soul Time. In general, ask yourself if an athlete in training would do "X" (stay up late, go to lots of parties, and so forth) and, if not, then neither should you. Some musicians like to gauge their activities before a performance by treating themselves as if they were ill.

Keep yourself on an even keel: two weeks before a concert is not the time to quit caffeine, if you normally drink it. Avoid starting new supplements or medications (unless your doctor deems it absolutely vital) or begin new habits.

At this point, your music should be so well learned, practiced and studied that you can practice just enough to keep in shape, but spend most of your time in score study and visualization. Perhaps you can devote some energy to conducting your music or dancing as described in chapter four.

Forty-eight Hours Prior

By 48 hours prior, postpone projects and meetings, if you possibly can. Until you have a lot of experience (and even then, if it is a high-stakes performance) be kind to yourself and lessen other pressures. In this regard, college and university students need to plan ahead. If you know that your big concert or recital will occur at the end of the term, talk with your professors at beginning of the term to see if you can avoid having projects and presentations at the same time. May you turn in work early or a bit late?

Spend your time studying your music, visualizing your performance, meditating, and journaling, supporting your mental and psychological process in the next few days. This is an opportunity to pamper yourself: take long walks, read good books, and watch silly movies. If you enjoy them, have a massage or visit a sauna, whirlpool, or steam room the day before, not the day of the event. Massages release toxins and you need time to flush them from your system and the massages, sauna, whirlpool, or steam room may make you a little too relaxed and rubbery to perform well.

At this point in your preparation, it is common to have some doubts and fears. If they arise, just remind yourself that it is normal. Take some deep breaths and do something that comforts you, such as taking a walk.

One thing I learned from reading Don Greene's books (please see Resources) is to have a carbo-load meal 48 hours prior to the performance—you will use this energy then. So if your concert is on Sunday afternoon at 4:00, on Friday at 4:00 have a nice big bowl of pasta or some other carbohydrate you enjoy.

By 48 hours prior, singers need to stay off the telephone and talk as little as possible. Even on cell phones we tend to use greater volume and higher frequencies, which can result in strain. You want to avoid speaking a great deal so that your voice feels fresh and rested. You can certainly email and text your friends. Even so, I would suggest that until you have several major performances under your belt, you isolate yourself a bit in general to help with focus and unflappability. That is true for instrumentalists as well.

Performance Day

Get as much sleep as you can, but certainly be up and alert at least two hours before any performance—to allow time for unhurried preparations. For singers it is vital to be up at least 90 minutes before you do any vocalizing, in order for the nightly edema and phlegm to drain.

Realize that you will have a major drop in energy on the performance day as your body and mind are marshalling their resources—so do not worry. Also avoid compensating with caffeine or carbohydrates, or you will be on the ceiling at curtain time! Make sure that any large meal is eaten at least four hours in advance, because you want your energy available for your performing, not taken up with digestion. You can, however, eat light things such as fruit up to the moment you walk on stage. Singers often like to keep fruit backstage and eat a bit in between groups of songs or time on stage, because the chewing and swallowing can be an effective release for the vocal mechanism.

The most important tip I can give you about physical and mental preparation on performance days is to suggest that you read on about keeping a log.

KEEPING A LOG

I came to graduate school as a late-bloomer surrounded by and competing with colleagues who had had years of voice lessons and performing experience. I was faced with a great number of auditions and performances and I puzzled over how I would determine what my body and mind needed before each outing.

I started keeping track of all the factors I could imagine that might influence my singing: how much sleep I had, what the weather was like, what I ate the night before (I would now add 48 hours prior), how I felt physically and emotionally, what I ate that day, how my voice felt ahead of time, what the hall was like, and then how I felt I did or if I received any feedback. Within a matter of a few weeks I was able to track patterns and build for myself comforting, supportive performance day routines, knowing how much sleep to get, what foods are helpful, and so forth.

What works for me is as unique to me as what will work for you. I urge you to start a log for yourself! Keep track of all performances and auditions, including informal performance classes, dress rehearsals (or even all rehearsals), noting all the variables listed in the log below--you might add your own categories as well. It can be especially helpful to give yourself a percentage from 0 to 100 compared to how well you normally play or sing the material. Keep in mind that many professionals consider that if one sings or plays in performance 75% as well as in the practice room, one is doing very well indeed! Track patterns and develop for yourself supportive, comforting routines.

An additional benefit from keeping a log is the psychological boon of realizing that every performance is only one in a series. This can help you develop a healthy detachment, almost a laboratory-style approach: "Hmm, this aspect didn't work so well for me this time. I wonder if I did thus and so what would happen in the next audition?" Maintaining objectivity can foster a sense of experimentation and play in your performing, which breathes in new life and creativity. Two variables that might assist in achieving this sense of exploration is the line for mental strategies used (please see chapter seven for more on mental strategies) and visualization or other preparations. Keeping track of your mental preparation and state, as well as physical factors, can greatly assist in developing long and short-term performance preparations.

SAMPLE LOG

Day, date and time

_____

_____

School/company/class/program

_____

_____

48 hours prior meal

_____

_____

Supper the night before

_____

_____

How much sleep the night before

_____

Physical state that day

_____

_____

Emotional state that day

_____

_____

Food eaten that day

_____

_____

Any stressors/surprises

_____

_____

Amount and kind of warmup

_____

_____

Weather conditions (humidity, allergens, etc.)

_____

_____

Outfit (including shoes) worn

_____

Audition space/acoustics/audition screen

_____

_____

Condition of piano/reeds/etc.

_____

_____

How I felt I did (percentage) _____ Comments

_____

_____

Mental strategies used

_____

_____

Visualizations or other preparations

_____

_____

Specific goal for this outing

_____

_____

Was goal achieved?

_____

Any feedback

_____

_____

Results

_____

_____

I AM ILL: SHOULD I STILL PERFORM?

This is a difficult question to answer, and yet another reason to keep a practice and performance log. Learning in low-pressure situations (small recitals, performance classes, studio recitals and so forth) what you can and cannot do under less than ideal situations is the best method for discovering how your mind and your body respond when you are fighting off illness. A serious illness requiring emergency care is certainly time to cancel any performing, as are situations involving fever, nausea, diarrhea, or when you are highly contagious.

However, a simple cold or the beginning or end of a virus might be possible to perform with. It would be wise to carefully assess your energy level long before concert time by beginning different movements or songs, recording yourself and/or getting feedback from your accompanist and trusted friends.

Most singers can perform with a head cold—in fact, some find it easier to track forward resonance because they are better able to feel where the tone should go. However, if the cold or flu is in the chest (and especially, if you are coughing) it is usually too hard on the vocal apparatus to sing and wiser to rest. The same is true if you have a bacterial infection.

LET'S TALK ABOUT PHLEGM

This section is, naturally, for singers although wind players might benefit from the suggestions as well. Phlegm does wreak havoc on everyone from time to time and certainly, when you experience mucus on your vocal folds in the middle of a performance, clear your throat. Habitual throat-clearing, however, actually creates more phlegm from the irritated vocal folds and surrounding tissues sending messages to the brain that they have been irritated—the brain then responds by sending more mucus!

Keeping oneself hydrated and healthy in general is helpful in reducing phlegm and singers need to think about respiratory health as part of their overall physical preparation and daily routine, not just at performance times.

- Pee pale, sing clear—the adage is true. If you drink enough water that your urine is pale in color, you are usually hydrating enough to slough off phlegm. Drink water throughout the day—most people can drink 2 liters without losing electrolytes (check with your doctor if you are concerned). Chugging water before a lesson, rehearsal or performance is of little to no value.

- As mentioned previously, rest is balm for the voice. Professional singers routinely sleep 10-12 hours before a performance!

- If you have morning rehearsals, practice sessions or lessons; get yourself up and alert well in advance—at least 90 minutes ahead of time. I would suggest 2 or 3 hours in advance, allowing time to exercise and

78

wake up your respiratory system, the opportunity for a nice hot shower --breathing in all that good steam)-- and time for breakfast so that your body is nourished to give you energy as you work and, also, by chewing and swallowing, you have warmed up many of the muscles involved in singing as well.

- Many singers use Guaifenisen, the generic name of over-the-counter (OTC) drugs such as Humibid, Tussin, Mucinex and so forth. It is especially helpful to those who suffer from allergies all year and to everyone in the winter, when phlegm thickens and lodges itself in airways and on your vocal folds. Guaifenisen is, in essence, a thinning agent and needs regular hydration to work well. Often what singers perceive as too much phlegm is simply phlegm that is too thick. Usually if you thin it, it will drain away. It is best to get just the Guaifenisen, without any decongestant or antihistamine—as those can be very drying.

- Another help for allergies and the drying effects of winter heating systems is to use a saline OTC nose spray. Check the label to avoid a lot of additives. When you are in a very dry environment, it can help a great deal to spray each nostril once an hour or so.

- Singers with allergies or colds often use a Neti pot. There are other versions as well—squeeze bottles can be somewhat easier to use. They also direct the water up to the small sinus openings, while the Neti pot just clears out the nose. You can make your own solution with a dash of baking soda, ½ t. non-iodized salt and 1 C. warm water, and then use an ear bulb to irrigate your nostrils. I do recommend, however, purchasing the ready- made packets to ensure purity and the right amount of salt--too little or too much can irritate your nasal passages. (Manufacturers of packets, squeeze bottles and Neti pots include Neilmed, Breathe-ease,

Saltaire, and Sinuaire.) It is also recommended that you use purified, boiled and cooled, or distilled water and heat it for just a few seconds in the microwave. Irrigation helps open stuffy noses, allows you to see if there is infection by the color, and lets any nasal sprays that you use afterward adhere to tissues rather than phlegm.

- An effective antidote for winter dryness and year-round allergies are those small, personal steamers. Use them from 5-20 minutes and you are more likely to have a productive cough and to breathe easier in general. Using a drop of vinegar or Eucalyptus oil can aid in opening the passages.

- Often young singers will drink lemon juice or hot water with lemon and honey—but that acidity is just as hard on the throat as clearing. Your body will simply send more phlegm to the area. It is much wiser to drink water, seltzer, water mixed with a bit of non-citrus fruit juice, and non-acidic herbal teas such as throat coat.

- Another reason for keeping a regular practice and performance log is to determine which foods give you optimum energy and which ones help create mucus. No two bodies are exactly alike: some singers avoid all dairy and wheat; others like to coat their throats before they sing by drinking milk.

- If your doctor prescribes antihistamines, investigate whether you can get them in a nasal spray form. Many otolaryngologists (ear, nose and throat doctors) believe that systemic antihistamines are too drying for singers. I certainly have found that high notes and agility are compromised by systemic antihistamines, although there are times and places when their use is absolutely necessary—when there is so much drainage that the whole vocal apparatus is compromised. In this and other vocal health concerns, it is always wise to consult an otolaryngologist who specializes in treating the professional voice. Ask your voice teacher, vocal coach and singer colleagues for recommendations.

- When you have a lot of phlegm and you are not in the middle of a performance, try swallowing, using a lot of air in a wheezer's cough, and then drinking water. Running rapid scales, changing between EE and AH vowels, especially in the lower part of your range will often help flick off the mucus.

- If after about 20 minutes or so of well-supported singing you still have phlegm, it may be that you are using surrounding muscles to help and it would behoove you to check with your teacher and be certain that you are supporting adequately and not "muscling" your singing (the tension is eased by phlegm). Or it may be that you are quite ill and it is time to rest your voice.

- A big producer of mucus is Gastro-Esophageal-Reflux-Disease (GERD) known generally as acid reflux. Contrary to what is depicted in television ads, most sufferers do not feel the burn and the majority singers have GERD simply because the act of support in singing helps to open the sphincter, allowing gastric contents of the stomach to travel up and inflame the surrounding cartilages. Otolaryngologists are divided about the percentage of singers affected: some say 80%, others 100 %. Usually the vocal folds themselves are not affected, but the cartilages that open and close them (the arytenoids) can become inflamed. Symptoms include having trouble with speaking and singing in the morning but getting easier as the day progresses, difficulty with higher ranges, a dry cough, a sensation of fullness in the throat, lots of thick phlegm.

Sufferers may have one or all of these symptoms. If you suspect that you might have GERD, please see your doctor and get on the appropriate medications and routines.

- Another producer of phlegm is actually from being overly concerned about the condition of the throat. Almost always, when we think too much about our throats and necks, we tense. That tension then radiates to surrounding muscles and tissues and, as in throat clearing, the irritation is soothed by the body in bringing more phlegm to the area! Unless you are very ill, you can almost always sing though some mucus. The more that you focus on calm breathing and support, the freer your larynx will be and the less likely to have phlegm.

Chapter Six

NURTURING THE ARTIST WITHIN

"Only when one is connected to one's own core is one connected to others . . .the core, the inner spring, can best be re-found through solitude."
—Anne Morrow Lindbergh

The Artist's Life

The life of a professional musician is one of great reward and satisfaction along with much sacrifice --this is also true of aspiring professionals and those still in training. If you are in school or beginning to build your career, you doubtless know the many forms of economic and social strain. Unless well-established or supported by others, most musicians live on a shoestring budget. Day jobs pay the bills and nights and weekends are not spent enjoying a fun social life, but in study, practice and applying for apprenticeships, grants and jobs. The strain can be felt in family relationships and the musician commonly lives with a sense of alienation: non-musician friends simply having no idea of the burdens of a music career. Because it can be such a challenging life, along with the unique demands of performing, it is essential to nurture oneself.

Most musicians face not only a lot of work and isolation, but also a fair amount of criticism and rejection. Non-musician friends and family cannot begin to understand this and anticipate your needs for love and acceptance, and colleagues are often caught up in their own struggles. So learn to practice self-love, rather than self-loathing. It may sound silly, but consistent rejection <u>does</u> build up in your soul, like a toxin does in your body and can result in a subtlety-increasing amount of self-criticism and dislike. So find ways on a regular basis to love yourself. That could take many forms and expressions. Perhaps loving yourself means taking an extra hour or an extra day off from work, study and practice one week. Maybe it will take the form of listening to some beloved music and making a list of all your best qualities and attributes. It could mean that you write a love letter to yourself: jotting down all the things you want to hear from friends, loved ones, teachers, even critics and judges. Loving yourself could include finding old positive jury comments, course evaluations, reviews, and notes or letters—reading them and savoring the praise.

Make time for fun, for recreation, and for renewal. The concept of a Sabbath, religious or not, might be helpful here. Yes, you must spend most of your time in practice, study, networking and so on. However, at least once a week treat yourself to an entire day or part of a day to relax and dabble in other pursuits. It may sound like just one more task to add to your long list as an artist, but it will help you reap great rewards in both creativity and longevity. Additionally, music is a form of expression and requires that you have something to express! If you spend every waking hour only on musical tasks, what new life and energy can you bring to this mode of expression? This is one reason why older performers are often considered more expressive than younger musicians—because they normally have more life experience to bring to their performing. Consequently, seek out new avenues of engagement: other arts, sports, reading or writing, volunteering in your community, the list is endless. If an entire day or part of a day off is just not possible, then take some Sabbath "moments" throughout the day. Meditating for fifteen minutes or taking a half-hour walk or reading one chapter in a good novel can be highly refreshing.

Several recent studies have shown that maintaining close friendships is essential to mental health and general well-being. Since so much of music study and practice is solitary, it is all the more important to enjoy social times and deeply connecting with loved ones and good friends, even if you cannot do it as often as non-musicians. Experiencing a multi-faceted, abundant life not only gives the performer greater depth, it also can help with a healthy sense of detachment. If you have a rich full life, you as an individual are not your singing or your playing—you are so much more than the sum of the parts.

Play

There has also been a lot of "buzz" in the media lately about the importance of play. Allowing yourself to play—in solitude or with others—will refresh you in deep ways, keep your mind sharp as you age, and give you more freedom in your performing and in everyday life. In fact, play researchers have discovered that play and sleep are both organizers of brain development and adaptability. That pliability can help you cope with all the curve-balls that life and performing throw your way.

Scientists have also learned that the very act of improvising in music—of free-wheeling playing, slows down the part of the brain involved in self-censoring—allowing for greater flow of novel ideas. That will happen with non-musical playing as well and carry over into performing.

What is play? Play is absorbing, making you unaware of time's passage. Play has no goal or end in sight. Play is FUN! Play might be blowing bubbles or seeing pictures in cloud shapes or rolling down grassy hills or talking to your dog. Play might involve others in making up a secret language or reading funny authors aloud or playing games such as charades.

Play is not trivial. In his book Play, psychiatrist Stuart Brown asserts that "The self that emerges through play is the core, authentic self." (*) He says that the truest expression of our individuality and our most alive, best memories come from times of play. It is also the way we remember others, especially the deceased. What fills the conversation at wakes and the time for sharing of memories at funerals? While work achievements and volunteer contributions may be mentioned, usually what is emphasized is the ways in which the person was fun, what she or he enjoyed doing, even his or her silliest moments.

Even so, as we mature, we are often made to feel guilty for playing. But, as Brown asserts, the opposite of play is not work, it is depression. Play and work are mutually supportive, sharing the quality of creativity. That is the reason why I have suggested, in other parts of this book, that you give yourself a zany practice session or one in which you simply tune in to the physical sensations of playing or singing and enjoy being in the moment and being one with the music.

Mr. Brown suggests taking your own play history. What did you simply love doing as a child? Was it alone or with others? How can you re-create that today? One way to invite non-directional play is to include animals and young children in your life.

Once you have given some thought to your own play history and style, take a playful approach to your music, your practice sessions, your other preparations and your performances Let play be your guide to greater joy and freedom.

Nurturing the Soul

Nurture yourself in deeper mental and spiritual ways. The aspects of mindfulness, fully inhabiting your body and living in the now that will aid in overcoming performance anxiety and attaining confidence will also nourish the artist's soul. But they are quite contrary to the prevailing western culture of multi-tasking, conspicuous consumption, living conditionally, and the belief that buying more things will create happiness.

As an artist, you must seek out your own inner path. Perhaps traditional religious practices will aid you on your journey. Maybe another discipline would be a complement to religious observations or a better fit for your unique spiritual quest. You might look into modalities such as Hatha Yoga, Meditation, Qi Gong, Reiki, and Tai Chi (please see the Resources section for more information). You will find your practicing more fruitful and the struggles of daily life more manageable by taking time to pamper your body and mind. Taking time on a daily basis to release tensions and feed your soul will reap great rewards in your ability to focus and to remain unflappable when mistakes happen in performance or other things do not go as planned. It is far less helpful to add a meditative discipline just before a performance, because then it has not had time to become a part of you.

Meditation

If you would rather be solitary in your pursuit of inner peace, start by giving meditation a try. Find a place where it is comfortable and quiet. Some individuals like to make a corner of their bedroom or office a little contemplative spot, with candles, flowers, inspiring pictures or books, perhaps a little electric fountain or finger labyrinth or Zen rock garden. All that is truly necessary is comfortable surroundings and quiet. You can be the most enlightened soul on the planet, but if your body is uncomfortable, you will not be able to meditate. Most people prefer to sit on cushions or on the floor, supported by pillows, but a chair can suffice as well. Take a few moments to breathe deeply and release the tensions of the day. You might try imagining that your mind is a chalkboard full of all kinds of markings that are your thoughts and feelings and memories of recent events–breathe deeply and slowly erase all those markings.

Breathing is a key component of effective meditation. You might experiment with the Yoga image of making a stack of golden coins: you breathe from the bottom up, even slightly raising your shoulders as your torso fills with air. Do this several times and then allow your breathing to be low and relaxed. It is the deep exhalation that then reduces stress. Another way to get the breath low in the body is to do alternate nostril breathing: plug your right nostril and breathe in through the left then out again through the left nostril. Next plug the left nostril and breathe in through the right and then again out through the right. Keep this going for several breaths until you feel your air going low in your body.

The next step is to lower your gaze, make it inward, think of soft eyes, or even close your eyes. Many people simply focus on the air coming in the body, the sense of expansion, and the breath leaving again. That might be enough to get you in a quiet place. If thoughts and feelings come up, simply acknowledge and release them, going back to your breathing. Other possibilities include lighting a candle and letting the flame consume all your attention or focusing on a flower or an inspiring picture. Whether concentrating on a visual focus or your breath, you might also add a mantra—make it very simple and meaningful. You may simply repeat a word such as peace or love or wholeness. Alternatively, you might chant part of a song or a prayer or a phrase that is important to you. You could sit quietly and see what comes up for you.

Some people ask someone to let them know when a set amount of time has gone by, or they set an alarm. It is not necessary to meditate for a long time. Many consider 20 minutes a day to be ideal but when you first begin, 5 might be just fine.

The Walk-Around

I learned this technique some years ago in an acting class. The underlying assumption is that by allowing all thoughts and feelings to simply exist, not repressing any of them, any internal chatter or mind racing is diminished as thoughts and feelings calm down and are released. We then feel more grounded, centered, and ready to go on with our day or our performance. It is important to practice this frequently and to do so when you are alone.

Walking in a circle at a normal pace, talk aloud and fill in the blanks of these phrases with short answers, preferably one word: I Am, I Want, I Need, I Feel. Give yourself several times for each category and repeat all four at least three times. You might contradict yourself, say bizarre things— just allow it all to come out. Similar to venting in a journal, you will feel some sense of catharsis. If you find yourself unable to come up with the next word, say, "I'm blanking" and go on to the next category. An example might be: I am a woman, I am a musician, I am a wife, I am angry, I am good, I am bad, I am blanking. The reason for speaking aloud is to keep yourself in the moment and avoid mind spirals; the walking helps the activity to be whole-brain and whole-person.

After some familiarity with the technique, attempt to make a real difference between the "I Want" and "I Need" category. Following several weeks of practice, you may be able to do this exercise silently in your head without speaking and walking, but if you find your mind wandering, at least walk. Having this tool "at the ready" is sure to help in difficult life situations as well as acting as an effective calming and focusing routine for backstage.

Jungian Active Imagination

According to Carl Jung's methods of analysis and understanding, we all have several archetypal characters within our psyches. The plan behind active imagination is to have an internal dialogue with these characters, to learn from them, to be free of their constraints at times and to come to peace with them. (I believe this is what Al Pacino meant in the interview mentioned in Chapter Two: freeing yourself for creativity.) For the purposes of performance confidence, probably the character most helpful to encounter would be the Critic, the Judge, the Editor, however you want to think of this part of your psyche (In his book, *The Inner Game of Tennis*, Tim Gallwey calls the unself-conscious, automatic doer Self 2 and the Critical voice Self 1.)

Active Imagination is not terribly esoteric or difficult to do and usually requires only a few minutes. Sit comfortably in a quiet area, perhaps with closed eyes or a lowered gaze. Breathe deeply and allow yourself to relax. See if anything comes up for you, in your mind's eye. You might even call the critic forward. Let your imagination go and soar—if you see a personage, ask him or her if he or she is the critic and, if so, what do they have to tell you?

If the critic is very brusque or unpleasant or if you have a whole group of judges, it may be wise to take a moment and breathe deeply. Perhaps do the flame exercise (below), so that you feel a sense of power and then come back to your conversation. Tell them you can use their help, their guidance, but not their judgment, condemnation, or criticism. See if there is a change in tone and if they have something in particular to advise you about. Ask questions, if you need to and end by expressing thanks.

You can even try active imagination while driving—because being behind the wheel can put you into the relaxed-yet-alert frame of mind. Once while driving I was thinking very critically about the issues that I believed a friend was not facing. Suddenly I had a very clear image in my mind's eye of an old woman—a crone, very old and very wise. She told me to focus on my own issues and leave my friend alone. I realized, a bit chagrined, that her advice was very good and thanked her.

Another variation is to use a journal at the same time—writing questions in your own voice with your dominant hand and use the non-dominant hand for feedback from your judges or critics. Perhaps drawing pictures along with writing words would stimulate deeper understandings.

SCRIPTED EXERCISES

The following exercises are written as a script that you could ask a friend to read while you close your eyes and practice the technique or you could record them yourself and use the recording as you practice. The indication of seconds in brackets is to let that amount of time elapse before continuing with the script.

Flame Exercise

With practice, this technique can help you feel relaxed and empowered anywhere. You might find a quiet corner backstage and do this for a just a few minutes and feel more grounded, centered and energized.

SCRIPT:

Sit comfortably with both feet on the floor and release your weight into the chair. Close your eyes and let your breath go ever lower in your body. [10 sec] As you continue to breathe deeply, allow your body to relax more and more fully and your mind to release all thoughts and concerns. [10 sec]

Keeping your eyes closed, move your attention to the center of your body, a couple of inches above your navel and about three inches in. This is your core, your center. In your imagination, see there a small flame flickering. [10 sec]

With the next few breaths, allow the air to fan the flame, so that you begin to feel warmth and energy filling your mid-section, along with a feeling of well-being. [30 sec]

With the next several breaths, allow that flame to continue to grow in strength—so that you feel warmth and energy all the way to the tips of your extremities along with an increasing sense of power and of being in the right place at the right time. [30 sec]

After you have explored your strength and your essence, allow the flame to go back to being just a flicker. Remind yourself that it is your essence and is available to you anytime you need it. [10 sec] When you are ready, open your eyes.

Touch-Response

This technique allows you to literally program yourself to feel relaxed and poised.
SCRIPT:
Sit comfortably, with both feet on the floor. Allow yourself to fully relax and release any thoughts or worries. Let your breath go lower and lower in your body. [5 sec]

See yourself in one of your favorite places, a very comforting and relaxing spot. It could be at the ocean, in the desert, the woods, the mountains, by a lake or brook or even your own back yard or patio or favorite room: any place that makes you feel safe and calm and peaceful. [10 sec]

Take a mental look around the place to capture every aspect: the smells, the colors, and the sounds. What makes it such a peaceful place—why is it particularly relaxing to you? [10 sec]

Fully experience the comfort and peace of your special place. Allow yourself to relax completely—feeling as if you were floating, enjoying a sense of ease and lightness. [30 sec]

Keeping your eyes closed, bring your attention back to this room and squeeze your first finger against your thumb—making the "ok" sign. Once you make the sign, go right back to your place and see all the details. [10 sec]

Repeat this coming back to the here and now, making your "ok" sign, and then going back to your peaceful place several times. When you are ready, open your eyes. [30 sec]

With regular practice, you will have fully programmed yourself and simply making the "ok" sign will help you feel relaxed. After some time, you can replace it with some other physical action, preferably one you can actually use in performance. For a singer, that might be pressing with your hands on the outside of your thighs. For an instrumentalist it might be curling your toes or pressing your knees together. Experiment to see what is both helpful and not easily perceived by an audience.

Yoga Deep Relaxation

This is the kind of activity that is most helpful in days leading up to a concert, in times of stress in general, and several hours before a performance—not immediately prior, as you want more energy and focus for performing than this will allow. The more often you use this tool, the more fully and deeply relaxed you will be. You might need a light cover or blanket over your body. Some people like to use an eye bag. If you suffer from lower back problems, you can lie on your back with your knees bent and your feet on the floor—in Constructive Rest position.

I learned this kind of relaxation from studying Hatha Yoga. It uses a Sanskrit word, *prana*, which means energy, life force, even love. If that word does not resonate with you, simply substitute energy or love or grace or peace.

SCRIPT:

- Lie down on your back, make sure your head is in a comfortable position, and relax deeply, let all your thoughts go [30 sec].
- Feel and relax the toes of your right foot, feel them grow warm and tingly. [5 sec] Relax your right foot and ankle [5 sec], relax your right knee and calf [5 sec], relax your right hip and thigh, and feel your whole leg melt into a warm ocean of *prana*. [10 sec]
- Feel and relax the toes of your left foot, feel them grow warm and tingly. [5 sec] Relax your left foot and ankle [5 sec], relax your left knee and calf [5 sec], relax your left hip and thigh, and feel your whole leg melt into a warm ocean of *prana*. [10 sec]
- Relax your pelvis and your abdomen. [10 sec]
- Relax the entire length of your spine, vertebrae by vertebrae. [20 sec]
- Feel and relax the fingers of your right hand, feel them grow warm and tingly. [5 sec] Relax your right hand and wrist [5 sec], relax your right elbow and forearm [5 sec], relax your right shoulder and your upper arm, and feel your whole arm melt into a warm ocean of *prana*. [10 sec]
- Feel and relax the fingers of your left hand, feel them grow warm and tingly. [5 sec] Relax your left hand and wrist [5 sec], relax your left elbow and forearm [5 sec], relax your left shoulder and your upper arm, and feel your whole arm melt into a warm ocean of *prana*. [10 sec]
- Deeply relax your shoulders. [10 sec]
- Relax your chest, especially the area around your heart. [10 sec]
- Relax your throat and neck [5 sec]; relax your jaw and tongue. [5 sec]
- Relax your facial muscles [5 sec]; deeply relax your eyes and your eyebrows. [5 sec]
- Relax your forehead and all the little muscles leading up to the top of your head. [5 sec]

- Check your body for any points of tension, and relax them. [5 sec]
- Now with each inhalation, imagine warm, white light entering the top of your head and with each exhalation, that light travels all the way down to the tips of your toes, relaxing and warming you. [10 sec]
- Feel your heart and from your heart send *prana* throughout your body [5 sec] and from your body, realize *prana* returning to your heart. [5 sec]
- Feel your heart and from your heart send *prana* to everyone near you [5 sec] and from everyone near you, realize *prana* returning to your heart. [5 sec]
- Feel your heart and from your heart send *prana* to the four corners of the earth [5 sec] and from the four corners of the earth, realize *prana* returning to your heart. [5 sec]
- Feel your heart and from your heart send *prana* to the sun, moon and stars [5 sec] and from the sun, moon, and stars, realize *prana* returning to your heart. [5 sec]
- *Om Shanti*, may you know peace. May the world know peace. When you are ready, touch the tips of your fingers together, and then bring them up to gently touch your eyes. Do a few easy stretches, and then turning on your side; use your arms to rise to a seated position.

OTHER AVENUES TO EXPLORE

Are you one of those people who cannot motivate themselves to meditate or try other relaxation techniques? Perhaps regular sessions of Body Mapping or Alexander Technique or Feldenkrais Method would be more helpful. Can you find a weekly Yoga class to attend or perhaps a Tai Chi session or maybe a Nia movement class?

I strongly advocate bodywork of some kind, because living in our bodies helps us to feel more grounded and centered and better enables us to live in the moment and avoid mind-spirals. However, if bodywork is completely unappealing to you and you suffer regularly from stage fright, you might look into other remedies such as hypnosis or acupuncture.

Similar to the benefits of the Walk-around described earlier, journaling can be of great benefit. You certainly can use this tool as you like: writing every day, or a few times a week or only when stressed or upset. There are also a variety of approaches:

❖ Writing a letter as if to a dear friend or loved one or God or a departed relative.

❖ Simply putting pen to paper (or hands to keyboard) and making yourself write for 10-15 minutes, even if the beginning is gibberish or comments such as "why am I doing this" or "I have nothing to say". If you try this method you might be surprised at what a powerful tool it is and you probably will be amazed at some of the insights and realizations coming out from the unconscious mind.

❖ You can also format the journal around questions, such as "What is my now?" "Where have I been?" and "Where would I like to be going?"

Some musicians like to take beta-blockers to overcome anxiety, but I suggest you avoid this avenue. Beta-blockers can be both drying and habit forming, they can exacerbate asthma and they occasionally keep performers from having the amount of excitement or edge they really need. If you feel you must try them, get the lowest dose possible from your doctor and be sure to experiment prior to the performance. I have heard endless tales of musicians experimenting with beta-blockers on the day of a big performance with disastrous results. They might simply calm you, but they also might make you feel spacey or disembodied or dazed. Be sure to try them in a rehearsal to see what the effect might be. It might be safer to give homeopathic medicines a try. One example is the Rescue Remedy from Bach Flower Remedies. Many performers find this natural, homeopathic tincture to be of assistance in feeling grounded and centered without any side effects. (www.bachflower.com) Again, acupuncture, hypnosis and therapy can be of great assistance.

(*) Brown, Stuart. Play. New York: Avery Books, 2009.

Chapter Seven

BACKSTAGE TIPS

"Great works are done when one is not calculating and thinking." --Daisetz T. Suzuki

"Over thinking is just another form of fear."—Queen Latifah

Preparing to perform while backstage is similar to the kind of routine that athletes use just before they run or skate or ski: the stretching, the dressing, the pumping up or calming down of energy, and the self-talk that "psyches" you to perform or compete. Most of the time musicians arrive in their performing clothes and, as suggested, having practiced in the performance outfit; those kinds of details are set. Below we explore the other areas, except the self-talk that will be covered in chapter eight. Practice these suggestions, especially the stretches and The Corner tips in your rehearsals so that they become a normal, reassuring and cheering part of your routine.

Arriving

✓ Arrive at least an hour before the performance time.

✓ Always allow ample time to get to the venue. The last thing you need is extra adrenaline from rushing around, backtracking from having lost your way, and worrying. If the place is unfamiliar to you, it might be wise to do a practice "run" the day before, making sure of directions, transportation to the venue and/or parking.

✓ Bring extra copies of your scores, to cover any contingencies. Sometimes accompanists rush from one gig to the next and music can get waylaid.

✓ Be sure to bring water, fruit or other light food, extra reeds or strings, lozenges, warm gloves, anything that will help you feel that you can deal with surprises.

✓ Greet your colleagues and then find a way to be alone. You might talk with your co-players ahead of time, just letting them know that you will need some time by yourself before you do any sound checks.

✓ Do not allow yourself to get caught up in backstage chatter as it simply drains and scatters you. It is a product of nervousness and feeds on itself—pretty soon everyone is breathing higher and higher and living less and less in their bodies, because it is a spiral of energy that frazzles.

Stretching

• Find a room or a corner of a room where you can be alone, and do some gentle stretches:

❖ Stretch with both arms way above your head and then sweep down to the floor, hanging like a rag doll. Keep the knees soft and breathe into the small of your back. Roll up from the base of your spine, so that your head is the last thing to come up.

❖ Do some slow and careful head rolls. Slowly roll your shoulders forward and then backward. Tense your shoulders way up by your ears and then release.

❖ Stand with your legs wide apart, knees soft. Open your arms wide and bring your left one up in line with your left ear. Bending to the right let your right hand go down to your knee. Stay there for a breath or two and then repeat on the opposite side.

• If you have not already warmed up, find a place to be alone and go at it slowly and meditatively—looking for the right coordination at first. If a trusted friend or teacher can come along and assist in your warming up, this can free your mind to be in a more flowing, meditative state, rather than having to be concerned that all the technical areas were covered.

• Now is the time to carefully review your scores or your list of technical and interpretive points for each piece. Hear the music in real time and allow the sweep of it to fill your body with energy and direction.

• You might bring an ipod or disc player or use your iphone or tablet to listen to your favorite artist—allow that inspiration to permeate your body and mind with bright expectation.

• At this point, assess your energy level. Most singers can have a fair amount of adrenalin because they rely primarily on large motor skills. For instrumentalists, even though you want the feeling and energy of your whole body playing, your fine motor skills usually require a lower adrenalin level. If your energy starts to feel too high, you might try the breathing exercises listed in "The Corner" below, or "The Walk around" or "Touch-Response" exercises described in Chapter Six. If, on the other hand, you are one of the few players whose energy is low before a performance, you might want to do some jumping jacks or other calisthenics or, perhaps, jog around the room until you can feel your blood pumping and your energy rising.

Checking In

At this point, check in with your colleagues and be sure that all is in order. If there are sections of duets or other chamber pieces that you would like to run, this might be a good time. It would also be an opportune moment for a sound check or a chance to adjust to the hall's acoustics, by going through the first few phrases of several pieces or movements.

Now make certain that the stage manager has all the information s/he needs, including stage set-ups, length of intermission, words of welcome and so forth. The stage manager, now, should become a backstage or green room guard, gently and politely keeping well-wishing friends and relatives out, as you and your colleagues, individually, prepare yourselves.

Remind them that you need some alone time, and find a corner, if need be. Chapter Eight will cover mental strategies that help you get in the zone.

The Corner

- Whether you use air to play your instrument or not, take deep breaths through your nose, to humidify the air. Think of releasing your abdominal muscles to breathe low, or imagine that you have gills in your back. If it is still hard to get the air low in your body, trying curling the tip of your tongue up to touch the ridge of the mouth, right in front of the uvula—that often helps the breath to deepen. Or you could try Yoga alternate nostril breathing: plug your right nostril and breathe in with the left, breathe out through the left nostril, then plug it and repeat the process with the right nostril. Repeat several times. Because we are aware of using just one nostril, we usually achieve calmer, lower breathing this way.

- Continue to do some gentle stretches: easy neck rolls, spiraling at the waist, stretching both up and down. Walk if you like, or sit calmly, but keep your focus and energy turned inward until it is time to go onstage.
- An additional reason for isolating yourself is that often well-meaning colleagues may offer last-minute bits of advice. If you have been diligent in all areas of preparation, you do not need new strategies or approaches—in fact, it may throw you off. Stay with what you have prepared.
- All the elements of preparation give you a solid foundation, a framework for your performing. Rather than being formulaic, this kind of methodical, self-initiated approach can, in fact, free you for great heights of creativity in concert. Imagine breathing the essence of you into your music, breathing new life into the scores as you play or sing.
- Check your body for any points of tension and release them. Be sure that your feet are fully connected to the floor.
- If you have practiced the alpha postures described in chapter four, do them in the last few minutes before you go onstage.

On Stage

Your performance begins the moment you enter the stage. Think of how a seasoned professional would enter, and let your head and your smile lead the way as you stride confidently onstage. Bow with your accompanist deeply, taking in the applause. As you are walking in and bowing and preparing, remember your job is to tell stories and move audiences. Do not impress—instead EXPRESS, in service to the music and the story.
- Make sure your feet are fully connected to the floor.

101

- Take a few moments to breathe deeply and hear the first few measures exactly the way you want them to sound. Stay with that ideal as your auditory focus.
- Singers, be certain to take a prep and come up as the character.
- Find your visual focus and stay with it.
- Whether or not you use air to make your music, imagine that you are breathing the audience in and blanketing them with your sound.
- If you make a mistake, remember the steps to quickly recover.
- Enjoy the applause and savor it with a deep bow. Even if you are not completely happy with the performance, take in the applause fully. You have given your gift to the audience and they want to thank you. Taking shallow bows, head bows or no bow does not look humble and contrite to the audience—it looks rude.
- Confidently exit and enjoy the fruits of your labors!

AUDITIONS

First, be sure to have your audition "package" fully learned, coached and performed many times. Perhaps you can get together with trusted colleagues and play or sing for each other, or practice presenting your audition pieces for friends, family, and church or temple members. Try out your pieces as many places and times as possible.

As with other performances, arrive early—at least 20 minutes ahead of your scheduled time. Often there is paperwork to complete and you want time to breathe deeply and become centered and grounded. It is generally a good idea to arrive warmed-up—often there are no rehearsal or practice rooms. You can follow the performance preparation suggestions above, such as stretching, deep breathing, score-study, and listening to music for inspiration—it all needs to be telescoped down into a few minutes.

If you run into friends and colleagues, smile and greet them, but ask if you can catch up afterward. Auditions can be filled with nervous backstage chatter that, again, will simply drain and scatter you. And there are some unscrupulous folks who, out of their own fear and self-doubt, might try to undermine your chances by planting fear in your mind through probing questions and scrutinizing looks. Get in a corner to be alone, if need be. In fact, many musicians think of those pre-audition moments as a time to pull inward, conserve energy and mentally protect themselves. Studying scores and/or listening for inspiration can be a great way to put up a protective barrier and get in performance mode at the same time.

Always bring extra résumés, headshots, and scores, as such things sent ahead of time can get lost. Provide your accompanist with front-to-back copies, no staples and no plastic sheet holders, please. Even those that are glare-proof are often too slippery for the accompanist to turn with ease. Mark tempi, dynamics and any cuts very boldly and clearly. If there are several cuts, unusual cadenzas, or tricky page turns, it might be wise to bring extra one-sided copies, so that the accompanist can spread pages out. It would also be smart to take a few moments and go over the cuts, repeats and tempi. If the accompanist starts at the wrong speed, simply stop and give a new tempo by singing or conducting it –never snap your fingers; that is considered rude.

When you enter the room, you are on stage: this can be the most important acting you do. With expanded posture, enter the room poised and energetic—as if you were a highly seasoned performer. Meet the judges' eyes, smile genuinely and greet them with warmth and friendliness. Normally they will ask what you want to play or sing. Focus slightly over their heads—in essence they want to be voyeurs of your performance.

Always start with your strongest piece, even if the person ahead of you just "nailed" it. Your performance is still valid, it is your interpretation. Never second-guess judges. If a singer has two arias in German listed on her or his repertoire sheet and one does not feel very good that day, oftentimes she or he will offer the alternative German aria, thinking, "Ah! That way the judges won't ask for the other." That kind of logic backfires many, many times.

The more you can look on your audition as a performance, the freer your playing or singing will be. Of course there is an element of judgment, but your job is to perform! In fact, the adjudicators normally want to see a highly polished performance. It can take some experience to get to this level of detachment, but the more you enjoy the process without caring about the outcome, the more infused with life and spark your performance will be.

Never apologize for your audition. If you are ill, do not try to "muscle" your way through—cancel instead. The music world is very small and you do not want to give a bad first impression. It is equally vital that you get word to the audition personnel—give them as much notice as possible and be certain they get the message. If need be, give a friend money for gas or cab fare and send a note in.

As far as audition results, one rarely ever knows. In German-speaking Europe, when singers audition for opera houses they are routinely given immediate feedback and suggestions for improvement. Unfortunately, that is not true here in the states. Sometimes you may be as perfectly prepared as the candidate ahead of you but because your appearance reminds the conductor of his or her "ex", you are not considered. Music directors and conductors often "go with a gut feeling" and that may be based on aspects of which they are not consciously aware. You have no control over that.

Conductors and music directors primarily rely on reputation, word-of-mouth information and recommendations. It is within your power to be a good colleague at all times, partly to keep yourself psychologically "clean," to "pay it forward" and also because you never know who might be hiring you or might be your next duet partner. Work hard and enjoy the process for yourself, and remember that the best revenge is singing or playing well. The universe will reward you, even if that particular music director or conductor does not.

Preparation for Ensemble Performances

1. Know your music! Study your scores at home: hear the music in real time, see if you can sense in your body what it feels like to play or sing the various passages. That way you are programming yourself for success.
2. Be aware that choirs often get very "chatty" in the last few rehearsals before a big event. It is from nervousness, but does not dispel the anxiety, and actually creates a spiral. Keep taking deep breaths, stretch breaks, and, especially, avoid talking.
3. For choristers, on performance days you may see orchestral members backstage chatting and joking, but remember that they have several minutes of reviewing tricky passages and so forth, while they await the conductor's arrival at the podium. This time of tuning and going over sections is a way for them to get in performance mode. Choristers do not have that tuning time onstage—you need to prepare to perform backstage. The same suggestions for rehearsals apply here: take deep breaths, do some stretches, look over your scores and avoid talking.
4. For instrumentalists, take extra time to tune and run a few scales or passages. Breathe in the essence of your instrument, become one with it. While you must listen for balance and sense of ensemble, it may be wise to think of yourself in your own swimming lane—working with the others but keeping your own counsel.
5. Trust the conductor: keep your eyes on her or him. If you feel anxious by seeing so many faces in the audience, do not allow your attention to wander from the conductor.
6. Savor the music! Enjoy the fruits of your labors. Breathe in the sound of the orchestra and/or choir; imagine that the music is coming through you. Feel the vibrations in your body. Giving into our senses not only increases the enjoyment but also stops the spiral of anxiety and helps us get back in our bodies and in the moment.

Chapter Eight

GETTING IN THE ZONE

"You are the music while the music lasts."-- T.S. Eliot

"The music happens between the notes." --Isaac Stern

This is the point towards which all of our previous work is aimed: getting into performance mode, aiming for a natural stream of energy, and, we hope, occasionally experiencing peak flows. Finding that energetic-yet-effortless flow almost never happens by thinking about it. Instead, musicians find ways to let go of expectations and to be truly in the moment. Below are a few ways to prepare ahead of time for getting into the zone, various last-minute tips and some mental strategies to try as well. I would recommend trying those last-minute tips and mental strategies with the laboratory-style approach of discerning what works best for you. Using your practice and performance logs or journals would also be of benefit here. Perhaps start with ones that appeal the most, or, alternatively, the suggestions that you would least like to try. It may be the case that you dislike certain ideas or approaches because they would require you to work on some areas of your life that need attention. In any case, feel free to pick and choose and perhaps change some of the recommendations or invent ones of your own.

Before the Performance

- Spending some time on the visualizations described in Chapter Two, the score study as detailed in Chapter Four, and regular performing-while-practicing will go a long way towards getting you in the zone. Then when you walk onstage, it is as if you have a movie running, and you simply step into it.

- Be certain that you are fully and thoroughly practiced and prepared. If you have taken your pieces apart and worked hardest on the challenging areas, if you have studied your music adequately and pinpointed problems, if you have mastered the technical and interpretive aspects enough that you can "go on automatic pilot," then you will be able to think about being grounded and expanded, breathing deeply, and your areas of focus. That will free you to get into the flow.

- Whenever you practice—whether for technical mastery or practicing performing—avoid being tentative. Sing or play at 75% of your available energy and sound. If you make mistakes, make big splashy errors that are easy to detect and correct. By playing or singing at 75% of energy, you create a sense of flow, a circle of energy with the audience, which allows no time to stop and worry. By the same token, playing meekly or tentatively will ensure exactly that kind of performance.

Last-minute Tips (practice in rehearsals and small performances before big ones)

- ✓ If you have a photo of yourself as a small child with a big grin on your face, gaze at it, breathe in the essence of that child who knew he could really perform well, or was sure that she could go out there and "knock 'em dead." Inhale deeply and remind yourself that the stage is a very safe place to let that spunky, confident child lead the way.

107

✓ Another aid is to keep a notebook of all the positive comments received from colleagues, teachers, critics and audience members. Maybe you have notes or cards from friends or even newspaper reviews. Look over all the good thoughts and reactions and remind yourself that you deserved all that success and certainly merit success now. Also take in the fact that the reactions were equally about how your performance affected him or her: the emotions felt, the catharsis experienced, the release from daily tensions. Tell yourself that the audience deserves to be moved and transported at the same time that you are worthy of being that conduit of love, energy and even bliss.

✓ For those singing operatic arias, scenes or entire works, during the last few minutes before you go on stage, start becoming the character, thinking his or her thoughts. This is where acting preparation comes into play. For every scene you are in, your character must have an objective and obstacle. For example, before Rodolfo in *La Bohème* first enters the stage, he is not thinking about shaky knees or dry mouth or butterflies. He is consumed with the artist's life—reveling in poetic thoughts. His objective is to get some writing done and the obstacle is hunger and cold. So you might try on the thoughts of "Oh, I like the light in our quarter today—perhaps I will attempt an ode to Parisian light. It is beautiful and yet it shows how barren the room is. I wonder if Marcello made any money today. What could we burn to keep warm? I cannot begin to think about food or my stomach will not let me write."

This kind of preparation can also work for songs. Perhaps you are beginning a recital with Purcell's *Music for a While* and you have spent some time creating a three-dimensional character to sing this song. Whoever your character may be, among his or her motivations certainly is the desire to entertain and to make the audience quite spellbound. So

108

thoughts backstage might include, "Ah! These people do not know what is in store for them! I will entrance them, mesmerize them, and give them an evening such as they will never forget! I can feel the magic overtaking me, filling me with energy and power. I will wait just a trifle longer to make their anticipation greater, and then TAKE the stage, like a tiger!"

- ✓ Play the part of a very accomplished performer. So often students respond to this suggestion with, "But they'll know what I'm doing!" Au contraire: you will simply look confident and poised. It may seem counterintuitive, but the more we play the part of a confident performer, the more confident we actually feel. As mentioned previously, one gimmick I frequently use in performance anxiety workshops is asking the performer to sing or play their piece again, imagining that she or he is a highly accomplished performer, playing for film. The sound will be dubbed in later—the performer must actually sing or play, in order for the dubbing to work. Almost always playing the rôle of an experienced, confident performer frees up the actual performing and sound in truly amazing ways!

- ✓ Similar to the thoughts for singing characters described above, you, playing the part of the seasoned professional can also have an inner monologue. It might be helpful to do a full character analysis and write out a few "scripts" ahead of time, or simply puff up your energy with deep breathing or the flame exercise and invent. One possible thought-stream: "Oh, it is good to be here, back in my home state. Of course, this audience will not be as sophisticated and fully comprehending as those at my last performance in Vienna, but it will be fun to dazzle them. I have performed this work so often that it feels like wearing a comfortable old shoe. Yet it continues to surprise me with hidden treasures. I can hardly wait to embrace this audience and share this rich music with them!"

✓ If possible, watch some athletic events the night before, or even back-stage, if you have the technology. Just take in visually, without analyzing too much, how runners or skaters or skiers prepare. Watch the competitors get into their zone—the flow of their performance.

✓ As mentioned in chapter three, humor can help to free us when we are feeling scared or stiff; it can loosen creativity and allow it free rein. Now you may think that all your technical and performance practicing and score study have led you down one secure path. While that work can enable smooth performances, allowing for new ideas and approaches, letting the creative fire burn can bring you to new depths of interpretation, to new heights of expression. So use whatever works to tickle your funny bone: read humorous books, listen to favorite comics on CD, or watch part of a DVD. Summon, within yourself, the intention to play.

✓ While you are taking deep breaths through your nose (to humidify the air) and doing some stretches, repeat a mantra over and over. *Again, this is something to work with ahead of time in practice sessions and rehearsals*: find a word or a phrase that helps you feel poised to perform and already in the feeling of the music. One way to make the mantra especially effective is to repeat it as you are listening to recordings of your music, or while studying your scores and hearing the music in your head. You can also repeat it to yourself while hearing the first few measures of each piece before beginning to perform. You might experiment with:

> o It's all mine.
> o I flow with the music.
> o I let go and let the universe play/sing through me.
> o Let.
> o Flow.
> o Permission.

- Take the stage.
- Let's play!
- Welcome to my party! (a lá Yo-Yo Ma)

Working regularly with a mantra in rehearsal and practice will ensure that it is an efficient tool in recovering from any mistakes or false starts. If you make a mistake, as mentioned before, accept it, tell critical voices to shut up, release body tension and let your mantra get you back into the zone.

Some Practical Suggestions

Sometimes just an idea or a tip can be enough to help us feel grounded and in control of the situation. Here are a few ideas:

➢ It may be obvious, but reed players should bring extra reeds and string players extra strings! So often I have found that that is not the case.

➢ Pianists are often helped by imagining that they are playing from their seat, from their behind. This usually helps with whole-body energy.

➢ Organists usually feel more power and centeredness by playing and balancing from their solar plexus.

➢ Singers with dry mouths/throats can get the saliva flowing by biting their cheek or tongue; or biting into an apple.

➢ Singers with very long programs or those worried about tension build-up, would be well served by keeping some apples or grapes backstage and chewing in between groups of pieces.

➢ A former colleague who is a fine jazz saxophonist mentioned that he always felt scared of getting a dry mouth or throat during performances until he started taking some water with him on stage. Just having the water there eased his nerves.

➤ Keyboardists and other instrumentalists often complain about cold hands in performance. A mental help can be imagining that a river of nourishing heat flows through the body from the middle of the forehead. Another help can be to keep thermal gloves and/or those instant chemical hand-warmers backstage. If you arrive without such aids, using warm water in the bathroom can be of help.

Mental Strategies

As previously mentioned, confident performing is highly psychological and dependent on finding the mental strategies and attitudes that work for you. One of the reasons I strongly advocate keeping a journal of all your performances and rehearsals, is to try different mind-sets and see what works well. That is another reason to ensure that many rehearsals are ones in which you truly perform rather than simply thinking technically.

Below are some points-of-view to try. It would be helpful to experiment with them in small performances or rehearsals, and if one is especially powerful, you could turn it into a daily meditation and write an accompanying affirmation. For example, let us say that the idea of flow and embracing the audience really works for you. Then you could spend a few moments daily imagining yourself onstage, filled with bright light that embraces the audience and circles back to you. You could mentally hear yourself play or sing during this brief visualization. You might alternate days of hearing yourself perform in the visualization with chanting a mantra such as "I am one with the flow of the music." The mantra would then be an effective trigger for in-the-zone playing or singing that you could use before each piece or movement and to recover from any mistakes.

* Take the risk; push the boundaries, BE FEARLESS. So often when we are precise and careful, we actually make more mistakes from being a bit tight. Let your body feel loose, go for that 75% of energy and think BIG in your performing.

* Consider your performance to be a natural part of who you are. You are already an artist; performing is as natural to you as swimming is to a duck. Ducks do not think about swimming, they never worry about it; they have no time for second-guessing themselves. Neither do you. You are as entitled to flowing, effortless performing as a duck is to swimming and quacking.

* As we explored earlier, our main job is to tell stories and move audiences. So throw yourself into your character or into the mood of the piece you are playing. Do not try to impress, EXPRESS. Impressing means you are thinking about the effect, and that takes you out of the flow. Expressing means you are one with the character, one with the music.

* If a particular outing is challenging your healthy sense of detachment, watch out the window to see a bus go by. That same bus will be going by at the same time tomorrow, no matter what happens in your performance. Life will go on and you are connected to it.

* Ask yourself: how would I approach this performance if I knew I could not fail? Imagine what that would feel like, how your body would let go of tension and expand. Breathe in that sense of power and permission.

* Getting in the zone, having that flow IS connectedness. Rather than stepping apart, at arm's length so-to-speak, practice in everyday life being one with your surroundings, one with the universe. (This is another

reason why I love the idea of breathing the audience in and covering them with your sound.)

❊ Think of your performing as a huge YES! Improvisatory actors and comedians often talk about the acceptance that needs to happen in improvisation. Even if the back-and-forth changes directions many times, or goes off into tangents, it is vital to always come from the feeling of YES. The minute one says NO, the flow and the improvisation are stopped dead.

❊ Some performers enjoy playing with the idea of having back-up singers, or a back-up band. It can be comforting to imagine a group supporting your every effort on stage. Practice this in rehearsals, so that your imagination is ready to fly with your "Pips" when in concert.

❊ Another take on a group of supporters, is to imagine spirit guides or angels holding you up, especially by the back of your ribs. Again, work with this in rehearsal so that it is a natural part of your performing.

❊ Embrace your audience, embrace the hall, embrace the music, embrace yourself and your colleagues, embrace the universe, and embrace life!

TIP: You ARE enough!!!

Chapter Nine

WHY DO ALL THIS? WHY BOTHER?

"After silence, that which comes nearest to expressing the inexpressible is music."-- *Aldous Huxley*

Sometimes following a workshop on overcoming performance anxiety, a participant will approach me reluctantly, even apologetically, and ask, "Why should I go through all this? Why should I add new disciplines to my life? Why do all this work?" My answer is always, "Because you deserve it." Dear Reader, please take in fully these words: you DO deserve it! Viewing this process as simply more work can be a thin disguise covering self-contempt. It buys into the idea that having performance anxiety means there is something wrong with you: that you are deeply flawed and somehow pathetic, not worthy of time and attention, not deserving of success.

Approach this journey as an opportunity to give something precious to yourself: time, attention and even healing and solace from the bumps and hurts and slights you have endured. This gift can provide great rewards both now and in the future in a variety of ways.

The various strategies for mental, physical and performance preparation will also be of value if your career path now or eventually centers on non-musical endeavors. Giving effective speeches or presentations calls for the same kind of poise, groundwork and energy as musical performances. Knowing how to prepare psychologically for big events or challenging audiences can be of great value to career mobility and trajectory. Certainly performing can be a highly charged experience. By gaining comfort and confidence in such a vulnerable undertaking, you are certainly poised to carry a great deal of confidence into everyday challenges.

Learning various strategies and techniques for living in the moment, truly inhabiting your body, even living meditatively will stand you in good stead within a culture that continues to grow in complexity. The stress of staying current in our cyber society, keeping up with numerous modes of communication and simply existing in a post-9/11 world can be overwhelming. No matter how often or even whether you perform, learning to slow down, to savor life, to enjoy moment-by-moment awareness can lengthen your life and give it much depth and sweetness.

Gaining comfort in performing can help one savor all that music can offer, including deeper insights into life itself. Music in general helps us make sense of things. Perhaps you have seen, via the Internet, the speech given by Professor Karl Paulnack, at Boston Conservatory, to students and their parents about the benefits of music making. He said, "The first people to understand how music really works were the ancient Greeks. And this is going to fascinate you: the Greeks said that music and astronomy were two sides of the same coin. Astronomy was seen as the study of relationships between observable, permanent, external objects, and music was seen as the study of relationships between invisible, internal, hidden objects. Music has a way of finding the big, invisible moving pieces inside our hearts and souls and helping us figure out the position of things inside us." I would add, if we actively participate in making music, it can help our psyches in deeper and different ways than if we simply listen. Paulnack continues, "Music. . .is not a luxury, a lavish thing that we fund from leftovers of our budgets, not a plaything or an amusement or a pastime. Music is a basic need of human survival. Music is one of the ways we make sense of our lives, one of the ways in which we express feelings when we have no words, a way for us to understand things with our hearts when we can't with our minds." *

116

Consider that music making adds beauty to the world, enriching both your own life and the lives of those around you—always a worthy endeavor. In fact, performing is participating in creation! Think of it: music as written is just black marks on paper. It takes the act of singing or playing to breathe life into a piece of music—and that life exists only as long as we sing or play. So even if you never compose a single line of music, or write a poem or paint a picture, by performing you are creating! Whether you desire a grand debut at Carnegie Hall, or you are happy to simply play some chamber music with a local group, being free of fear and able to fully relish playing and sharing music can help make this world a little bit better.

Making and listening to music is a powerful way to experience the Celtic idea of a "thin space" –the eternal shining through time and space and the intersection of our material world with another, deeper dimension of reality. Affording these sacred moments for yourself, your fellow musicians, and your audience is a generous and even holy thing to do and therefore worthy of time, sacrifice and effort. A poem I wrote, describes it this way:

THE SINGING LIFE

I never sing in the shower.
My song is meant to be shared.
A risky exposure of self
Prodding, stirring up
unspoken dreams.

A fleeting glimpse,
A moment of knowing
there *is* a greater something.
Communion of singer and listener
transported
to a life of the spirit
where rapture awaits.

Your ability to free yourself of stage fright and wholly enjoy and share deeply with others can benefit everyone by creating, at least for a little while, a greater sense of community. Music's ability to both create and under gird community is mighty, indeed! A rowdy crowd at a ball game becomes unified in singing patriotic songs. Guests at a wedding turn into participants simply by singing a hymn together. Divisiveness is diminished and commonality is raised by chanting together in worship. And because we <u>are</u> the instrument (or an equal partner to it) as well as the player, we bring much of ourselves consciously and unconsciously to our performing. Making music together allows us to grow in many subtle and even mysterious ways, making our ties ever stronger.

Simply listening to music can be therapeutic. If you rid yourself of anxiety, and are able to perform from your core and share with others, the healing in mind, body and soul can be profound, indeed. Again I quote from Professor Paulnack at Boston Conservatory, describing what happened in New York City on 9/11: "I observed how we got through the day. At least in my neighborhood, we didn't shoot hoops or play Scrabble. We didn't play cards to pass the time, we didn't watch TV, we didn't shop, and we most certainly did not go to the mall. The first organized activity that I saw in New York, that same day, was singing. People sang. People sang around firehouses, people sang *We Shall Overcome*. Lots of people sang *America the Beautiful*. The first organized public event that I remember was the Brahms *Requiem*, later that week, at Lincoln Center, with the New York Philharmonic. The first organized public expression of grief, our first communal response to that historic event, was a concert. That was the beginning of a sense that life might go on. The US Military secured the airspace, but recovery was led by the arts and by music in particular, that very night."

Choosing to make music, to overcome nervousness so that performing and sharing is a regular part of your life, can help not only you but also those around you, in important ways. Again, quoting Professor Paulnack: If there is a future wave of wellness on this planet, of harmony, of peace, of an end to war, of mutual understanding, of equality, of fairness, I don't expect it will come from a government, a military force or a corporation. I no longer even expect it to come from the religions of the world, which together seem to have brought us as much war as they have peace. If there is a future of peace for humankind, if there is to be an understanding of how these invisible, internal things should fit together, I expect it will come from the artists, because that's what we do. As in the Nazi camps and the evening of 9/11, the artists are the ones who might be able to help us with our internal, invisible lives."

So please aim to conquer your anxiety, work on these strategies and techniques because you deserve it, as it will make your life deeper, fuller, richer, since it will help you make sense of things and release stress, and because the world deserves it! Making music with and for others is far from a selfish, vainglorious pursuit. It very well might, as Paulnack asserts, save us.

A CAVEAT AND A QUOTE

I generally close my workshops with a caveat and a quote. First the caveat: if after trying several of the techniques explained here for a few weeks or months, perhaps reading another book or two, or trying a workshop, you find that it is getting no easier, please pay attention. If you are not improving or the nerves are getting worse, that usually means the performance anxiety you experience is symptomatic of some deeper psychological issues. That was certainly right in my case and seeking out help and working on my issues gave me a whole new life—truly!

Often folks will say, "Oh it will cost me an arm and a leg and I will be in therapy forever!" First, you merit the attention and the help; you are worthy of a rich, full life. Secondly, there are clinics in most locales that provide psychotherapy on a sliding fee scale and some that are free. There are also clergy who are trained and will offer their services for no charge. (Please see Resources section for more information.) And, finally, the length of therapy literally depends on how hard you work on your issues—in addition to private sessions; you might seek out 12-step groups or support networks as well. Please consider giving yourself a loving, life-changing gift!

The quote is from Marianne Williamson's book, <u>A</u>

<u>Return to Love</u>:

Our Deepest Fear

Our deepest fear is not that we are inadequate.
Our deepest fear is that we are powerful beyond measure.
It is our light, not our darkness, that most frightens us.
We ask ourselves, "Who am I to be brilliant, gorgeous,
talented and fabulous?"
Actually, who are you not to be?
You are a child of God.
Your playing small doesn't serve the world.
There's nothing enlightened about shrinking so that
other people won't feel insecure around you.
We were born to make manifest the glory of God
that is within us.
It's not just in some of us; it's in everyone.
And as we let our own light shine,
we unconsciously give other people permission to do the same.
As we are liberated from our own fear,
our presence automatically liberates others.

* Quotes from Paulnack speech used by permission.

120

Chapter Ten

THE HELP OF ALEXANDER TECHNIQUE

"The method of the Alexander Technique is not one of remedy; it is one of constructive education.—John Dewey

In the chapter on physical preparation, Sharon stated, "Because singers ARE their instruments, and instrumentalists' bodies are certainly equal partners, bodywork of all kinds can be beneficial." This chapter focuses entirely on one of those methods, the Alexander Technique. The Technique provides a method for giving attention to your use, attention which is sorely needed in our Western civilization that has emphasized the separation of mind and body, and the use of mind to the exclusion of body. This use of mind and neglect of the body helps to feed performance anxiety.

What is Alexander Technique?

Felix Matthias Alexander, an Australian actor suffering from laryngitis, recovered the use of his voice through several years of self-observation, and began teaching his findings in 1894. Through meticulous observation, he realized that his rehearsal and performance habits included gripping the floor with his feet and pulling his shoulders up and back, causing an over-arching of his spine. His over-arched spine increased the tension in his neck, thereby pulling his head back and down onto the top of his spine, which he termed *downward-pull*. All of this misuse had placed pressure on his larynx, and resulted in hoarseness and vocal strain. Any of those habits sound familiar?

121

Do what Mr. Alexander did, and sing, speak, dance, while observing yourself with several mirrors that allow, as in a dressing room, for views of your sides and back.

In addition to identifying the habit of *downward pull,* Mr. Alexander discovered that downward pull's antidote was accessing what he termed *Primary Co-ordination;* our inherent mechanism for balance in the body. He realized, through his methodical observations, that it is possible to co-operate with and facilitate the Primary Co-ordination of our psycho-physical *Self.* He called this choice, *Constructive Conscious Control.* And the method for making a different choice, he termed *Inhibition,* often called *The Pause* today. An explanation of its use follows later in the chapter, and you will have the opportunity to pause in your reading and practice it. After pausing from habit, the Alexander Technique student or practitioner has the opportunity to give themselves *Directions,* inviting a different response to the stimuli of everyday living, the stimulus of a live audience, or the stimulus of fear symptoms.

Alexander Technique teachers, in the process of instructing students in the use of the principles, provide hands-on instruction. This hands-on teaching is useful in re-training the kinesthetic sense, our movement sense. Our kinesthetic sense gives us information about our body: its position, its size, and its movement. In Don Greene's focusing techniques, which were described in Chapter 2, Mental Preparation, he encourages that attention be given to your kinesthetic sense by noticing the breath coming and going. The Alexander Technique invites this breath awareness as well, along with a re-education of the entire psycho-physical person or *Self.* With guidance and instruction via "Alexander hands," we can return to our inherent balance and ease, which is always available to us. The one-on-one work with a teacher is important, and resources for finding a good one can be found at the end of this chapter. In the meantime, there is much you can explore on your own, and there is a great deal you can accomplish by changing your thinking and perception of your position, size, and movement.

Let's Explore:

- Begin by attentively watching an infant raise her head from a belly-on-the-floor position, and you will see Primary Co-ordination at work. The infant/toddler has not yet learned to interfere with this inherent mechanism.
- Observe the movement of a cat and you will see the basic principle of Primary Co-ordination in all of its graceful glory.
- You can recover this movement sense by cooperating with it, intentionally, whenever the thought crosses your mind. It is the return to balance which is important, NOT finding this balance and attempting to freeze it in place, thus producing tensions and holding patterns in the body. The struggle to hold oneself in place is called "good posture." We will not be pursuing that goal. Just keep coming back to your ease and freedom. Be willing for something new to emerge, a recovered way of being in your body, as you sing, speak, stand, sit, and walk.

As my mentor and teacher, Barbara Conable, wrote in her book, How to Learn the Alexander Technique, "You voluntarily, 100% on purpose, cooperate with your intrinsic, inherent, vital support." And how do we cooperate with this support? Dale Beaver, Alexander Technique teacher at The Ohio State University, tells his new students, "The Alexander Technique is all about how you move and how you think about it. It's all about your thinking; it's not about your doing."

BODY MAPPING YOUR PLACES OF BALANCE

How to think about ourselves? First and foremost, we must have in our possession an accurate mental map of our body, and a basic understanding of its places of balance. Mapping our structure assists us in discerning our balance and ease. We begin our explorations with Body Mapping, developed by Andover Educator's founder, Barbara Conable. What we are accessing with our mapping is the dynamic relationship of the head, neck, and torso. This relationship organizes our movement and alertness. When gravity can travel freely through a balanced body, a partnership between earth and body can occur.

The primary place of balance in the body is where head and spine meet. Let's organize a search-party for this primary place of balance:

> "Anatomy-speak" for the meeting place of head and spine is the "atlanto-occipital joint." Palpate (feel with your finger pads), for your occiput (the knob at the back and bottom of your head). IN from there is the A/O (atlanto-occipital) joint. This primary place of balance in the body is located between your ears and behind your nose.

> Let's continue this mapping by placing thumb pads in front of ears, right where you can feel the knob of the jaw joining the skull. Touch the tips of your two middle fingers together. Travel around the head to the knob at the back, the occiput. THAT'S your head! That is what balances on the spine. Please note: the jaw was NOT included in our exploration of head. The jaw is an appendage, and when we attempt to balance it on the spine, along with the head, we will find ourselves out of balance, instead of in.

> Another way to find this essential balance place in your body is to travel with the tip of your tongue from the ridges of the hard palate back to the place where the palate becomes soft. Just above this change from hard to soft palate is where the atlas (your first vertebrae) meets the base of your skull. Play with a bit of head nodding, first a gentle, rocking "Yes" motion, followed by a quiet and slight, "No" movement. Allow this movement to initiate at the joint, which is interior, and does not require extrinsic muscle involvement. The muscles "come along for the ride," but they are not the start of the movement. Your A/O joint, and the small muscles that attach to it, are what get you started on all that bobble-head motion.

TIP: When this balance place is aligned, the rest of the body will happily follow.

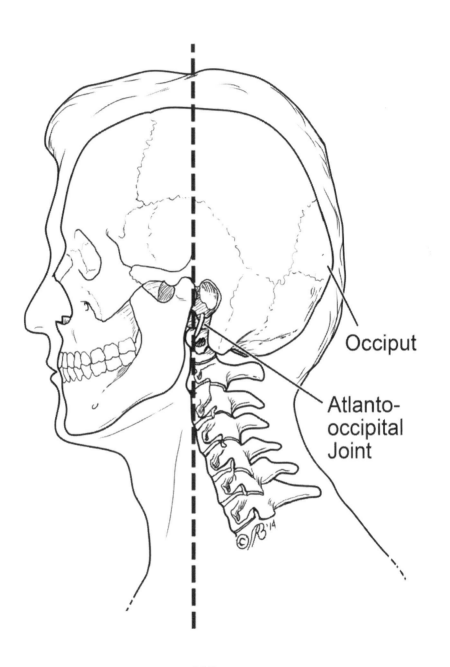

Occiput

Atlanto-occipital Joint

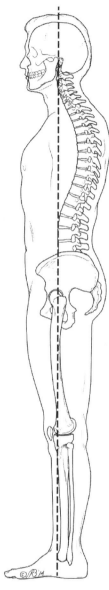

     As you read through these descriptions of the other balance places, keep in mind that our thinking must always return to head on spine. Knowing how the rest of your structure balances is helpful, but head on spine takes the optimal- use prize! Keep inviting ease and movement at this joint, and all of the other places of balance will have an easier time finding theirs.

Find thyself an anatomy book. Find thyself a most excellent anatomy website. These are my favorite books: <u>Albinus on Anatomy</u>, Robert Beverly Hale and Terence Coyle, and Frank H. Netter's <u>Atlas of Human Anatomy</u>. Pour a cup of tea, and direct your curiosity to the intricacy and marvel of the human body. Please, please, and pretty-please locate a side view of the spine first. Prepare to be amazed. Curves! Four of them to be exact. Sinuous! Snake-like! The posterior (back) or anterior (front) views of the spinal column will not reveal the curvaceous structure of your body's core. Feast your eyes on the side views and let your spine have its curves. Your body will thank you, because it is so much work to try to make the spine so straight when it is so very curvy.

As stated previously, now, and forevermore:
The primary place of balance is: head on spine.

The second place of balance is the head and thorax on the lumbar vertebrae.

As Mr. Alexander observed in his own use, the head is often forward of the thorax (the chest cavity, containing lungs and ribs and heart), especially in today's world, as we use our computers and devices. Our eye gaze results in our heads moving in the direction the eyes take. Once the head is balanced over thorax, these two can rest comfortably over the lumbar vertebrae. The lumber vertebrae are the bottom five vertebrae of the spine. They are massive and curve deep into the pelvis. They support the head and thorax merely by being there, not by any excessive muscular effort on your part.

Third place of balance is torso over legs.

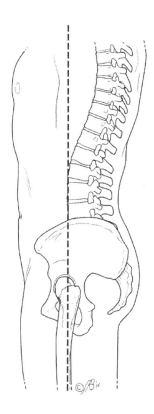

Ah, we come to the hips. And this requires a pause to consider the fantasy of THE WAIST. Contrary to popular opinion, you do not have one. No one has a waist. It is a clothing word. It describes the band around the top of a skirt or pair of pants. It is not a body part or a body place. As we think, so we move? Yes. We will attempt to move, to breathe, to live, as if we have this phantom place in our bodies. And this imaginary waist is often considered to be the MIDDLE of the body. Well. The mid-point of your body, head to toe, can be found at your hips, not at your fantasy waist.

Yes, I did write hips, and I do mean, hips. Find where the hip joint resides in you, and this change in your body map will alter your use in a dramatic and wonderful way. Remember the palpating with fingertips to locate your occiput? Now, you can palpate once again to find your hip joint. It's lower than you think. From standing, the best way to find it is to place your thumb in the crease of your pants, which appears when you lift your leg off the ground. That's hip. That's halfway. Above is torso/head. Below is legs/feet. The mass of bone which you can feel along the side of your hips is the greater trochanter. (Get that anatomy book out! Look! See!) The joint itself, where the ball of the femur meets the socket of the pelvis, is deep in the body, not on its surface.

Fourth place of balance is at the knees.

Knees have three positions. They are: bent, locked, balanced. You can guess which one is recommended for your daily and performing use. How to find balance? Do the opposite of what you think should be done, and lock those knees. Yes, lock them. Then....release, ever so slightly, and there is your balance at the knees. We often attempt balanced knees by bending them, and that only creates extra work for the knees and the legs and the feet.

Fifth place of balance is the arches of the feet.

Each foot has three arches, and they form tripods. Think music stands! There is an arch across the ball of the foot. From the ball to the heel are the two other arches. We are most familiar with the arch along the inside of the foot, and many of us wear shoes to provide support for it. In addition, we have an arch from the ball to the heel along the outer side of the foot.

When you are considering these arches, be sure to map them meeting at the middle of your heel, not along the back of your heel. Support is always interior. Why do these arches matter?

Remember the maxim, "As you think, so you move." Thinking of arches will provide you with buoyancy and balance.

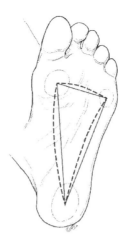

Sixth balance place is arm structure over the torso.

A practice to assist you in balance of arms over torso is to imagine your torso as the window, and your arms as the drapes. Draperies are fluid and moveable fabric. See the open window, and the drapes lightly dancing in a breeze. Those drapes are your arms. They are not holding the window up, nor do they support the window. They adorn the window. Let your arms drape themselves around your torso, and give them a break from the un-needed work of attempting to keep you upright.

Arm does not begin at the "shoulder." The first arm joint is where collarbone (clavicle) meets breastbone (sternum). We move arm from there. Try this: initiating the movement from your fingertips, raise an arm out and up, the other hand's fingertips resting on the meeting place of sternum and clavicle. Notice the movement at this first joint of the arm. Second joint is where upper arm bone meets the shoulder blade. Thirdly, arms move at the elbows, and lastly, at the wrists, a complex marvel of eight different bones that permit subtle variations of movement.

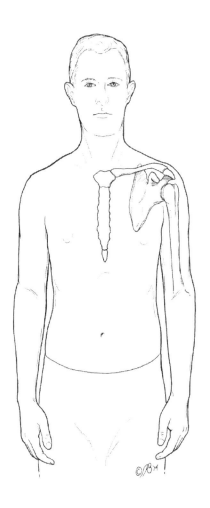

THE PAUSE, WITH PROMPTS

   With a more accurate body map, we can move into movement with a splendidly balanced body. The Alexander community practices the Technique utilizing what is called, "Thinking in Activity." In a lesson, a teacher will guide the student through basic everyday movements such as sitting in a chair, moving from seated to standing, moving from standing to seated, walking, raising arms, etc. Give yourself a reading break right now, and think your way through moving from sitting to standing. Notice, I wrote "think." This is also called *The Pause*, or in Mr. Alexander's vocabulary, *Inhibition*. We have the impulse or the thought to move, and instead of an immediate response, we observe how the body responds to the mere thought of moving. This can be a powerful practice, as it becomes clear how an impulse to move can initiate a cascade of tension and undue effort.

All right. So you've noticed your body's responses to your thought of moving from seated to standing. Now, give yourself the invitation to follow-through with the thought to move, engaging your *Self* (mind and body) fully in the business of moving. Often, a mental prompt will be of benefit, and these are some of my favorites:

- *"I allow myself to move forward and up, that my spine may lengthen and my torso widen."* (That's directly from Mr. Alexander, and has been in use for decades.)

- *"Head leads, body follows."* (Always a good choice.)

- *"Think up."* (That's up with the head, and not from the top of the head, but from the interior joint where head meets spine.)

- *"Feel the feet."* (This is a great way to return to the body after having left it behind in a bout of mental exertion, or nervousness, to the exclusion of body awareness.)

- *"Free the neck."* (Just a thought; not a doing.)

- *"Whole-body, whole-world."* (A favorite at central Ohio's Capital University.)

These prompts, in Alexander Technique lingo, are called *Directions*, and their use is elemental to the practice of the Technique. Give them a go. Make up your own. Know what

133

each word means to you, and let your directions take you into movement, into life, into the very best performance that is in you.

THE WHISPERED "AH"

"As we think, so we move." Breathing is the body in motion. If we think the ribs are doing the work of breathing, our bodies will attempt to initiate movement at the ribs, even though it is not possible. If we try to make our diaphragmatic muscle move, the body will do something else instead, in yet another attempt to follow this incorrect thought. To clarify and define where and how we move for breathing means that we can cooperate with our body's functions instead of fighting them.

As you read, give a portion of your attention to the breath patterns of your body. It is breath that produces sound; spoken and sung. The flow of air traveling up through the trachea on exhale sets the vocal folds to vibrating, that wee pair of muscles nestled behind the thyroid cartilage. In men, this cartilage is often visible and is referred to as the "Adam's apple." Palpate with your finger pads at your throat, while lightly humming. The place of greatest vibration is the location of your larynx.

Take the phrase, "rib cage," and throw it into the trashcan. Click Delete. A cage has bars. A cage does not move. Ribs do. Ribs follow the gentle ebb and flow of the lungs. They move up and out on inhale, down and in on exhale. Ribs move at joints, which attach all along the vertebrae at the back and the sternum at the front. Muscles between the ribs, the intercostal muscles, lengthen and contract.

Abdominal muscles, of which you have four sets, release on the inhale, and move back toward the spine on the exhale. The diaphragmatic muscle extends the full circumference of the torso, dividing the lungs and heart from the viscera (all of your other internal organs). It looks like a pizza dough round being tossed in the air by a chef. The diaphragm does its work best when the singer is free of tension and holding, so that it can move without restriction. And move it does. Although it is believed to do the greatest percentage of the work of breathing, we have absolutely NO voluntary control over this muscle. None. Return to the balance of head on spine if you wish for your diaphragmatic muscle to serve you well. Optimal use in the rest of your structure will permit the diaphragmatic muscle its full excursion as it domes and raises on the exhale, and slightly flattens and lowers on the inhale. Get out of its way!

Inhalation is the body's response to exhalation. On the inhale, the body re-bounds; the body responds to the exhale. The inhale is not something the body DOES; the exhale is the "work" of the breath process. And neither the inhale nor the exhale has a starting or stopping point. Consider the waves on the beach. As you sip your coconut beverage, the water laps the sand, but at no point stops before receding back into the sea. So our breathing.

Learning to trust this pattern of letting the breath come in, rather than taking it in, requires time and patience and practice. Mr. Alexander, in the early days of his teaching, was known as "The Breathing Man," and he wrote extensively and passionately on the perils of the then-popular breathing exercises used in what were called "Physical Culture" programs. In response, he developed a simple way to re-educate breathing habits. It is called, *The Whispered AH*. Not to be confused with a stage whisper, this tool is a profound exploration of the muscle elasticity required for efficient and easeful breathing. The challenge is learning to use an unprepared inhale.

1. Begin with this acronym, "TTTT," which stands for "Tip of Tongue Touching Teeth." That's the tip of your tongue lightly touching the backs of your bottom teeth.

2. With the thought of a smile, the corners of your mouth slightly lifted, release the jaw and speak/sing/whisper an "ah" vowel. If you choose the whisper, it is imperative that it is a barely discernible sound. Anything more will be too much air pressure on the vocalis muscles.

3. And here's the part that really matters. Observe. See what happens next if you simply wait. The breath will return. It must. And when you can be present to that

moment when the body's reflex kicks in, and <u>gives</u> you the inhalation, that's a moment of discovery. You may find that the sound stops before the next inhalation needs to happen. Let the breath rebound in its own good time. Renew your acquaintance with the elasticity of the breath pattern, and breath-holding will no longer interfere in your daily life or in your performing.

The Whispered AH offers practice with the foundational Alexander Technique concept of *Inhibition*, introduced at the start of the chapter, and explained in the section on prompts. Further clarification of this concept will be useful to your Alexander Technique explorations. Although Mr. Alexander was a contemporary of Sigmund Freud, they used this word "inhibition" very differently. In the world of psychotherapy, it is understood to be a word to describe repression of emotion or excessive reserve. In Mr. Alexander's usage, inhibition means stopping. It is the choice to desist, to refrain, to stop from using habit. Instead, we pause to see what might emerge in place of our habit. And with The Whispered AH, what shows up is the next free and easeful inhalation!

CONSTRUCTIVE REST

And now we pause, in fine Alexander Technique fashion, to explore another AT practice----*Constructive Rest.* CR was originally designed by Mr. Alexander's teachers-in-training. They would prepare students for a lesson with FM by guiding them through this practice. It is also called Active Rest, Semi-Supine, or an Alexander Lie-Down. Lying in a semi-supine position, (on the back with the knees bent and feet flat on the floor) direct your neck to be free, so that your head can release and your spine lengthen and widen. It is as simple as that. 10 minutes, 20 minutes, even 5, will give you the benefit of an altered relationship to gravity in the midst of a busy day, and provide you with practice in *"non-doing."* You set up the conditions for a bit of ease and comfort and then remain alert to notice the effects.

Certain details are helpful. A yoga mat on the floor is best, as it provides a firm surface. One or two books may be placed under the head, if you find any discomfort at the head and neck without that support. Books are used instead of pillows. Hands may rest palm down on your abdomen or arms outstretched with your palms up. Many AT teachers have recordings of directions to listen to while in Constructive Rest. My favorite is Lilly Sutton's, *Guided Constructive Rest: a Lesson in Self-Care.* Please see her website, LillySutton.com, and click on Guided Constructive Rest for ordering information.

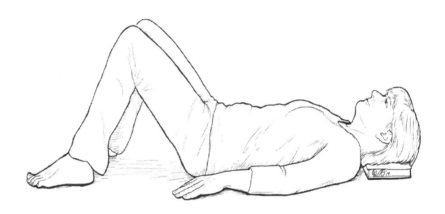

INCLUSIVE AWARENESS: NARROW FOCUS AND WIDE FOCUS RE-VISITED

Flip or scroll back to page 22 and re-read Sharon's section on "Narrow Focus and Wide Focus." "The ideal, over time, is to play or sing in a way that is more inclusive of the audience." What follows is a delightful way to access and invite this inclusivity. With a narrow focus being attention to our bodies, our "other" and our ideal sound, wide focus includes all

137

of those plus everyone and everything else. Overwhelming? At the beginning, yes. "Learning to stay grounded and undistracted with a wider focus can take several months to do." That's Sharon again, from page 21. And, indeed, when presenting this practice to a new student who was preparing for a show, she reported that she wasn't quite ready for inclusion of her audience. She needed more time with the narrow focus challenges. How wise of her to notice this, number one, and secondly, to tell me! With that caveat, you can make your own choice about when to use this protocol, which student Sophie Stokes and I created. Sophie joined my teaching studio with an interest in both the Alexander Technique and singing. We had been working together for about a year when we collaborated on a protocol for healthy vocal tone production. This protocol emerged out of her weekly lessons, and reflects her openness to being present in the moment. Sophie walked in the door "with a couple of things" one day. . .a desire to sing with more volume, and the wish to project her sound without pushing or creating un-needed tension. As I listened to Sophie, I remembered bright mornings at Seven Oaks Retreat Center in Virginia, when Dale Beaver would start our day of Alexander Technique study with The Six Directions. North, South, East, West, the sky above, and the earth below, were each, in their turn, saluted by us, using chant and gesture. Greeting each day on the grasses of a wide meadow gave us a communal and individual experience of inclusive awareness.

With this memory as a springboard, Sophie and I crafted the following. We invite you to play with this sequence of directional thoughts. For our purposes, we used the verb "sing," but you could just as readily speak or move to the directions. If you select to produce sound, take responsibility only for the making of it, and NOT for the sending of it to each of the six directions. Sound, once produced by the body, leaves the body, and cannot be hurried along. Breath sets into motion the vibratory pattern of vocalis muscles, which in turn produce waves of sound. Done.

- Inviting "soft eyes," sing with attention to the front of you, including everything out to the horizon. Imagine what is beyond your actual sigh-line, and sing gently to that: 5-4-3-2-1 on AH.

- Sing with thought to all that is behind you, your unseen world. You are, in Alexander Technique parlance, "building a back." Visualize what is out-of-sight in the "backness" of you. Vocalise: 5-4-3-2-1-2-3-2-1 on AH.

- Engaging your peripheral vision, sing with your sides, and all that encompasses your "sideness." Think out to what enlarges your side-world. Vocalise: 1-3-5-3-1-2-3-4-5-4-3-2-1 on AH.

- Sing while including all that is under you, feeling the support of the floor and the support of what lies beneath it (earth, sediment, rock, lava). Vocalise: 5-slide to 1, then 5-4-3-2-1 on AH.

- Sing, being cognizant of what is above you, through the roof, to the sky and endless space above. Vocalise: 1-3-5-8-5-3-1 on AH.

- Sing, speak, move with all six directions in your awareness: up, down, side, side, back, front. Invite your inclusive awareness. See in your mind's eye the Leonardo DaVinci drawing of the Proportions of Man, with arms and legs outstretched. In your thinking, take this two-dimensional drawing into three-dimensional space, experiencing your Self in a sphere of spaciousness.

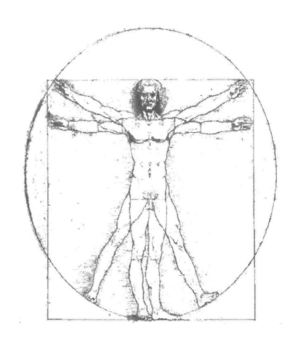

PERFORMANCE ANXIETY AND THE
ALEXANDER TECHNIQUE

In my own experience of using the Technique to enhance performance, I have primarily benefited from giving myself something else to think about and tend to, besides the "symptoms" of fear. Instead of a cascade of physical catastrophes to magnify further through my attention, I give my thinking to my use, starting with an awareness of feet. This grounds me in my surroundings and takes me out of my head and into the place of body WITH mind. It really isn't one or the other, the body misbehaving and the mind scattered, but often the "corrective" is to <u>first</u> include the body in my awareness and thought, because I have taken a mental "flight of fancy" into fear. The mere thought of "Feet" gives my feet back to me, and I can often identify imbalance in the three arches of support which the feet provide. From there, it is up and up to the primary place of balance in my body, the meeting of head and spine, between my ears, and behind my nose. A simple thought for this primary balance dramatically alters my experience of being in my body. Thoughts of feet and of head balanced on spine are not thoughts to the exclusion of the body's physical responses, but are invited alongside an ongoing acknowledgement of each unpleasant fear symptom. You had a chance to practice inclusive awareness through The Singing Six, and here is a real-life application for it. Fear and balance. Shakiness and supported feet. Sweaty palms AND a balanced head on spine.

STORIES: MINE AND ANNE'S

In my early 30's, I was diagnosed with thyroid cancer. The thyroid glands were removed in a surgical procedure which sometimes results in changes to the voice due to nerve damage. In addition, this surgery was followed by several radioactive iodine treatments. Having been a singer and a student of music all of my life, this was a sobering setback. My singing had always come naturally to me, and prior to the time of the surgery, I had sung happily without giving much thought or attention to how I did it. In fact, I was among those who purported to "not want to think about it too much." Well, all of that changed when the cancer diagnosis was given, and the surgery took place.

A whole new world of possibility opened up to me when a teaching colleague suggested the Alexander Technique as a way to recover my singing and speaking voice. Two years passed as I worked faithfully to restore my voice and overall health, and I was able to return to singing employment in the fall of 1993. Oh, joy! At long last, I was back to what I loved, and the primary vehicle for recovery of my voice and health was the Alexander Technique. I studied with Barbara Conable in her private teaching studio, and also with Lucy Venable at The Ohio State University. I also attended several OSU Winter Workshops on the Technique, organized and led by Bill Conable, retired OSU cello professor. Martha Munro, currently a theatre faculty member at the University of Pretoria, South Africa, was then living in Columbus with her husband and son while her husband completed his doctoral studies at OSU. I learned so much from her use of the Alexander Technique and the Feldenkrais Method as she coached me in recovery of my voice. Karen Peeler, DMA, now retired from the OSU School of Music, was instrumental in my decision to open a teaching studio.

Because of its amazing benefit, I remained keen to continue studying the Technique, even after my voice had been restored. Encouragement and training from long-time mentor and teacher, Dale Beaver, along with teacher-training intensives through Robin Gilmore's Chesapeake Bay Alexander Studies and Martha Fertman's Philadelphia School for the Alexander Technique, resulted in completion of required training hours. With sponsor support from Alexander teachers Meade Andrews, Robin Gilmore, and Bob Lada, I became a certified teacher of the Technique in the summer of 2012.

Reading about the Technique is fascinating and informative, but even more so is finding a teacher with whom to study and learn. My certification is through Alexander Technique International, and you can find teachers in your geographical area by visiting their website. Word-of-mouth is always a good choice, too! Central Ohio, where I live and teach, has a plethora of good Alexander Technique teachers, and students have their pick from many qualified instructors. The Cincinnati area has a dedicated and devoted professional group of Technique teachers, most of whom have been certified through AmSAT (American Society for the Alexander Technique).

Anne Johnson made her living as a professional singer in the 1980's. Since then, singing has been her avocation and her therapy. It is an important avenue for expressing her emotions and conveying her thoughts on the world. In 2005 and 2009, she had major surgeries, both times in the same area of her neck. The first was to remove her thyroid glands and the second was to fuse two herniated discs in her cervical spine. The latter surgery rendered her hoarse for six months and Anne found that she was unable to speak much above a whisper, let alone sing a note of any kind. To further complicate the issue, in the fall of 2009, she required a third surgery in the cervical spine to remove the hardware that was stabilizing the spinal column. A year following these surgeries, Anne began Alexander Technique and voice studies with the hope that she could begin to build some strength and stamina in her speaking voice. At this point, singing again was not even on her radar.

Through this work, Anne was able to regain not only her full speaking voice, but was able to sing again and in a range that she had not been able to sing in for years. This work was so successful that in January 2013, she was able to perform a two hour cabaret show with her former singing partner. I attended the show both nights to provide hands-on Alexander Technique reminders, both prior to the show and during intermission. Anne's voice remained strong and unwavering throughout both performances. "This was truly a miracle for me," she said. "I thought my days of singing were over. I cannot believe the impact that the Alexander Technique had on my voice---it was truly amazing." Anne and I have gone on to become cabaret show partners, and are currently working on a new show.

BOOKS:

Albinus on Anatomy, Robert Beverly Hale and Terence Coyle. Paper. Dover Publications, 1988.   This gem of an anatomy book is primarily for artists, and is designed to aid the art student in "observing more clearly than ever the shape and position of bodily forms." Albinus, the greatest anatomist of the 18th century, gives the Alexander Technique student an aesthetically pleasing view of the body in motion.

Atlas of Human Anatomy, Frank H. Netter, M.D. Paper. Ciba Pharmaceuticals Division, Ciba-Geigy Corp., 1989. Netter's successful career as a medical artist has made this book the premier "go-to" tome for anatomical accuracy. An invaluable resource for the student who is interested in all the anatomical details!

Body Learning, Michael Gelb. Paper. Henry Holt & Co., 1994.

An excellent introduction to the Technique, with numerous anecdotal accounts of its use. What Gelb calls "the operational ideas," also known as "the basic principles," are clearly defined in this accessible and entertaining book.

Guided Lessons for Students of the Alexander Technique, N. Dawley, N. and V. Schapera and M. Wilker. Paper. Four Winds Press, 2010. For students seeking homework assignments, this photo-rich workbook provides many practices for exploring the Technique. It includes practical applications for everyday activities such as using the computer, carrying a bag, and driving a car.

How to Learn the Alexander Technique, Barbara Conable. Paper. Andover Press, 1995.
A classic for the Alexander Technique library, this is the primary text for university and college-level Alexander Technique courses, and is required reading at The Ohio State University. Outstanding.

Indirect Procedures: A Musician's Guide to the Alexander Technique, Pedro De Alcantara. Paper. Clarendon Press, 1997.
A more advanced treatment of the Technique, this would be a good choice after reading Michael Gelb's, *Body Learning*. De Alcantara has a useful section on practicing, and also includes a chapter titled, "Stage Fright." Well-worth your while.

The Use of the Self, F. Matthias Alexander. Paper. Orion Books, Ltd., 1988. When this book was first published in 1932, the *British Medical Journal* called it a classic of scientific observation. Prose style of writing did not come easily to Alexander, but the content of the book is essential reading for the serious Alexander student. Wilfred Barlow introduces the book, succinctly describing FM's work as being "concerned with the intimate management of our moment-to-moment perceptions of ourselves."

What Every Musician Needs to Know About the Body, Barbara Conable. Paper. Andover Press, 2000. This spiral-bound primer is an illustration-dense compilation of Barbara's body mapping instructions and encouragements. Her light-hearted tone gives the reader a playful introduction to the basics of body mapping.

WEBSITES:

www.alexandertech.org (American Society for the Alexander Technique)

www.ati-net.com (Alexander Technique International)

www.balanceandharmonyat.com (colleague Jennifer Roig-Francoli)

www.bodymap.org (Andover Educators)

www.dianamcculloughstudios (get information on up-coming workshops and clinics)

www.jessicawolfartofbreathing.com (good resource for body mapping of breath)

www.LillySutton.com (site for purchase of Guided Constructive Rest)

Diana McCullough, voice and Alexander Technique teacher maintains a studio in Columbus, Ohio and is a clinician at regional universities and colleges. She recently launched a Cabaret show with former student, Anne Johnson, and she co-facilitates The Confident Performer Workshop with her colleague, Sharon L Stohrer. Please visit her website at: https://sites.google.com/site/dianamcculloughstudios/home

RESOURCES

Books on Practicing, Auditioning and Overcoming Performance Anxiety:

Art of Practicing, The by Madeline Bruser. Paper. Bell Tower, 1997. Subtitled: A Guide to Making Music from the Heart. Making music with your whole self, enjoying practicing, savoring music moment by moment: these and other concepts are presented to re-kindle our love for music. Not waiting until just before a performance to think of expression and emotion, but bringing our whole selves to our practicing makes the journey more enjoyable and reduces performance anxiety as well. Well worth reading.

Audition Success by Don Greene. Paper. ProMind Music, 1998. Subtitled: An Olympic Sports Psychologist Teaches Performing Artists How to Win. I found this to be highly readable and informative. The book simply chronicles the story of two musicians (a French Horn Player and a Mezzo) as they prepare for auditions and performances. The transcribed conversations are chock full of ideas to apply to one's own practicing and preparation without the over-pedantic style of many books on this subject.

Fight Your Fear and Win A 21-Day Plan by Don Greene. Cloth. Broadway Books, 2001. Subtitled: 7 Skills for Performing Your Best Under Pressure-at Work, in Sports, on Stage. I would read either Inner Game of Tennis or Soprano on Her Head to start the process/journey of working on performance anxiety. I think this book is for someone who has already worked on some performance issues and is ready for a real "battle plan." Includes a seven skills profile (determination, energy, perspective, courage, focus, poise, resilience) and a website for scoring the quiz. Then one is equipped to focus in on only those areas that need improvement, with plenty of ideas and approaches for improvement.

Inner Game of Tennis, The by W. Timothy Gallwey. Paper. Random House, 1974. A Gem! There's a reason this book has been in print for over 25 years. You needn't be an athlete to profit from Gallwey's suggestions. It is easy to draw mental parallels with performing and the book is an enjoyable read, to boot.

Performance Power by Irmtraud Tarr Krüger. Paper. Summit Books, 1993. Currently out of print, but worth looking for. Dr. Krüger is both a psychotherapist and a performer (organ) with lots of information to give on the manifestations of performance anxiety physiologically and psychologically. She also offers good preparation techniques, relaxation exercises and even some "quick-fixes."

Performance Success, by Don Greene. Paper. Routledge, 2002. As with *Fight Your Fear* (above), this book includes a skills profile and a website for scoring the quiz. It, too, is a 21-day plan but this time focused on getting ready for a performance and overcoming anxiety along the way. The reader is asked to find a mentor and to participate in a rigorous and structured plan. This may be a great approach to take before a high-stakes event: a debut or a senior recital.

Soprano on Her Head, *A* by Eloise Ristad. Paper. Real People Press, 1982. The BIBLE, really. Don't be fooled by the title, it's for instrumentalists, actors, dancers, all performers. Great ideas for practicing, preparation and performing. I have often given copies of this book to non-performers, because, as the subtitle says, it is *Right-side-up reflections on life and other performances.*

You Are Your Instrument, by Julie Lyonn Lieberman. Paper. Huiksi Music, 1991. Written for instrumentalists as well as singers, this book is full of fresh ideas--not re-hashing all the other books out there. Especially useful are ideas for using the whole person in practice and integrating both right and left brain hemispheres in performance. Very different from the other books on this list and worth a read-through.

 # Body Work Information:

Feldenkrais Method
www.feldenkrais.com/
Feldenkrais Method® improves movement, relieves pain.

Group Centergy
http://bodytrainingsystems.com
Centergy is a combination of yoga and pilates using breath with movement to make the body grow longer and stronger. It incorporates athletic training for balance, mobility, flexibility, the core, and helps reduce stress.

Massage
Look for information online or ask for referrals. A licensed massage therapist is often a better choice than large massage centers. Many offer reflexology, shiatsu, myofascial release, and trigger point therapy.

Nia Movement
www.nianow.com/
Original creators describe the technique, and offer a regional directory, newsletter, testimonials and FAQ.

Pilates
www.pilates.com

Pilates.com features comprehensive information about the Pilates Method, including equipment, videos, books, history, training, studio locations and more.

Rolfing
www.rolfing.org

What is Rolfing®? Find a Certified Rolfer in your area. Rolfing training and continuing education for bodywork practitioners.

Shiatsu

A traditional hands-on Japanese healing art, Shiatsu can help in a wide range of conditions from specific injuries to more general symptoms of poor health. Many trained massage therapists offer it along with traditional Swedish massage and other modalities.

Tai Chi
www.americantaichi.net/

Comprehensive and reliable information about the health benefits of Tai Chi and Qigong. Hosted by American Tai Chi and Qigong Association.

Yoga

There is so much "buzz" these days about Yoga, that few sites offer basic information. You can always check *The Yoga Journal* in your public library or online at www.yogajournal.com. For local classes, check YWCAs, YMCAs, Community Parks and Recreation websites, community college continuing education classes, and public high school continuing education courses. You can also try searching online with "yoga" and the name of your city or town.

Energy Work Information:

Acupuncture/Acupressure
www.acupuncture.com
Rich in resources on Traditional Chinese Medicine, acupuncture, Chinese herbal medicine, qigong, tuina, dietetics, diagnosis and theory,etc.
As with Yoga, you can also find a wealth of material by just searching with acupuncture or acupressure and the name of your city or town.

Meditation
Like Yoga, there is a wealth of online information about various forms of meditation. For classes and groups, look at YMCAs, YWCAs, extension classes, brochures and newsletters on alternative modalities available at health food stores, and Yoga centers.

Qi Dong
Unlike Reiki or some other modalities, there is no central or world-wide organization for Zhineng Qigong. As with yoga and meditation, look in continuing education resources, alternative newsletters and reiki or yoga centers.

Reiki
www.reiki.org
Non-profit organization offers classes, newsletter. Includes library, class schedules.

151

Psychological Help:

Hypnosis

www.apmha.com
National Hypnosis Association for Licensed Medical and Mental Health Professionals, National Referrals for Hypnosis Treatment

Psychotherapy

www.apa.org
The American Psychological Association (APA) is a scientific and professional organization that represents psychologists in the United States. APA educates the public with information on all kinds of disorders. Website has a link to find psychologists.

www.psychologytoday.com
Website includes a link to find local therapists.

www.aapc.org
American Association of Pastoral Counselors has information and a link to find local therapists.

ABOUT THE AUTHOR

Sharon L. Stohrer is on the voice faculty at Capital University in Columbus, Ohio. She previously taught for New York University and the College of Saint Rose in Albany, NY. Sharon also teaches privately, works with musicians and speakers on overcoming performance anxiety and co-facilitates The Confident Performer Workshop with her colleague, Diana McCullough. Please visit her website: www.sharonstohrer.com .

Made in the USA
Charleston, SC
28 October 2015